THE SOFT SKILLS HANDBOOK

EMPOWERING YOUTH FOR CAREER EXCELLENCE

VIRENDER KAPOOR

ATLANTIC

PUBLISHERS & DISTRIBUTORS (P) LTD

ATLANTIC
PUBLISHERS & DISTRIBUTORS (P) LTD

7/22, Ansari Road, Darya Ganj, New Delhi
Tel.: +91-11-4077 5252, 2327 3880
E-mail: orders@atlanticbooks.com
Web: www.atlanticbooks.com

Published by Atlantic Publishers & Distributors (P) Ltd 2024

Disclaimer

- The author and the publisher have taken every effort to the maximum of their skill, expertise and knowledge to provide correct material in the book. Even then if some mistakes persist in the content of the book, the publisher does not take responsibility for the same. The publisher shall have no liability to any person or entity with respect to any loss or damage caused, or alleged to have been caused directly or indirectly, by the information contained in this book.
- The author has fully tried to follow the copyright law. However, if any work is found to be similar, it is unintentional and the same should not be used as defamatory or to file legal suit against the author.
- If the readers find any mistakes, we shall be grateful to them for pointing out those to us so that these can be corrected in the next edition.
- All disputes are subject to the jurisdiction of Delhi courts only.

Printed & bound in India by Atlantic Print Services

Preface

"Competition is always a good thing. It forces us to do our best. A monopoly renders people complacent and satisfied with mediocrity".

—Nancy Pearcy

Today, young graduates passing out of college struggle to get a job. The job market is not good, and no government can contain a lack of employment every year despite all political promises.

There are over a hundred applications for one simple, not-so-great job, and people try all sorts of tricks to land a job. The actual struggle starts now.

It is like an actor getting his first break. They are lucky to get the first role. Even if it is a big banner, you need to deliver it so that your picture does well. You need to keep giving successful films, if not super hits, to merely survive.

The job market is in a similar situation. You land a job—Congratulations! But it is more important to retain the position. The earlier you understand this, the better it will be for you.

I would not stop short of retaining the job—that is defensive. It is like boxing; you don't want to play defensive, and you need to hit out. Should you be content with just chugging along like a *musafir* or a passenger on a train? Nah, if that be so, you may be asked to get down at the next station.

I have been briefing my students from a management institution at Symbiosis and several others on how to do very well at a summer internship and get a job offer from the company for their performance.

It was a complete session for the batch before going for their project. Those who paid heed got a job offer, and others who did not do as briefed returned empty-handed.

Let me tell you that a student has just two months to showcase their worth over there. And in that window, almost twenty per cent of students get a pre-placement offer (PPO).

These are simple things that need to be done to excel in an organization, most of which are based on attitude.

Let me say it loud and clear: Companies hire based on qualification and aptitude but fire based on attitude.

This book will show you how to, but you and you alone have to play the game. This book is your friend, philosopher and guide. This is not a motivational book; it is a book that tells you what to do and what not to do and motivates you to do your best.

It is not about retaining a job but about becoming a star performer, an asset to the organization they would like to retain, maybe forever, and get faster promotions.

There is no rocket science, and you don't have to be a Bruce Lee-like champion or a boxer like Cassius Clay to beat your competition. These simple ideas have been working for my students for decades and are very much achievable. So grab it.

Virender Kapoor

Contents

Part 3: Be Great at Work

Introduction

Toppers Alone Don't Do Well in Life

"*It will never rain roses: when we want to have more roses, we must plant more roses*".

—George Eliot

I have been dealing with GenNext for the last twenty years as a director of a management institute at Symbiosis University and thereafter helped establish another B-school in Pune, Maharashtra. I interviewed more than eight thousand graduates (B.Com, B.A., B.B.A., M.Sc, B.Sc), hotel management graduates, engineers, and so forth during these years. In addition, the interaction with more than two thousand parents has also given some important inputs. Since the eligibility criterion for an MBA was graduation, I have been able to grasp the shortfalls in our education system very well and now know 'why graduates in India are unemployable'.

Several studies have brought out that most graduates, when they pass out of college, are unemployable. Those from top colleges alone can hope to get a job, whereas more than 6.5 million graduates pass out every year, which also includes 1.5 million engineers. Graduation is the worst hit in our education system. There is neither any rigour nor any worthwhile academic curriculum. The quality of faculty is poor or, at best, average. Commerce and arts students don't even attend classes; studying a week before the exam is only good to get reasonable marks but not good to get a job.

The result is that a graduate is likely to have very limited basic domain knowledge for which they have primarily enrolled themselves. On top of it, they have no other 'skills' that are required to get employment. College, therefore, neither gives them the skills that are essential for employment nor any domain knowledge.

The worst is that since there is no one to guide these students, they end up doing nothing on their own and waste the three to four years of their 'prime time'. They all are between eighteen and twenty-two years of age, bubbling with energy, and yet unable to find a direction. The majority of the parents have no clue as to how to guide them. This not only happens in small or tier-2 towns but also in metros!

I have seen thousands who transformed themselves from being mediocre to becoming extraordinary performers. I have also seen people losing a lifetime opportunity and who missed the boat to glory and success. Why do some succeed, and why do several fail? Then later in life, some become 'haves', and most remain 'have-nots'. There are many reasons for this, which need to be explained and explored.

I realized that most graduates, when they come out of college, are not only unemployable but also directionless.

In fact, they did very little during their schooldays, too.

Their friends, too, are sailing in the same boat and cannot be of much use. If one does a rough calculation, the impact on the national resource is mind-boggling: 6.5 million multiplied by three years comes to 19.5 million youth man-years that are wasted on a regular basis.

It is not the fault of the students. This is a systemic problem. But if the system is not good enough, a student has to find a way to move forward in life, make a good living, work confidently and move up the ladder—whichever ladder he wants to climb.

> *"A lot of people never use their initiative because no one told them to".*
>
> —Banksy

This book will give you all that you need. But hard work has to be done by you.

You have to ask yourself a few hard questions.

1. Do I want to be successful in life and make a good living for myself?
2. Am I prepared to listen to the advice given in this book and take corrective actions to move forward?
3. Have I utilized my time productively, or have I wasted my time until now?
4. Am I prepared to start now to make a change in myself?

Having answered these truthfully, make a resolution that you will now read this book and follow the directions given in each of the chapters.

Remember, most young boys and girls have great potential and can do very well in life. You must not underestimate yourself.

I have been counselling youngsters on 'how to gainfully utilize their time during graduation' and also what they could have done from class eleven onwards in school such that they would have been better prepared for life.

How they could have spent their time more fruitfully so that they were ready to seek a job as a graduate, ready for interviews and competitive exams by enhancing their skills on their own. During these gruelling counselling sessions, most of them felt that they did not do the right things and their present situation was because of that reason. Almost all of them said that no one told them to do things that would benefit them. There was no guidance either from the colleges or from their parents.

If one would leave out the top forty or fifty B-schools (who get top-class graduates) and look at several below these and compare the performance of their students, one would realize that the colleges below the top fifty that have 'some additional zing built into the curriculum' do much better than those who don't. This invisible zing is the differentiator between a good and a bad B-school in that cluster. And this zing is designed to bridge the gap between a good and a bad graduate. Therefore such management institutes struggle to bring these 'unskilled, poorly educated half-baked' graduates first to a reasonable level of competence and motivation, and then start teaching management curriculum.

Let me emphasize that 'toppers alone don't do well in life', provided they can work on 'other areas' that can compensate for their diminished academic performance. Remember, everybody cannot be academically bright. But everybody has a right to live with dignity, good money and a reasonably good lifestyle.

The reverse is also true: Many toppers and gold medalists also don't do well in life. This is because they also do not have the skills that we are going to discuss in this book.

Let me put it straight: This 'zing factor' takes an engineer from an annual remuneration of two hundred thousand to four hundred to six hundred thousand. The zing factor makes you employable and gives you the confidence to move on in life without a crutch. I always say, 'Management is more vocational than educational,' and this zing covers the vocational portion.

I have turned around students who were weak academically, had very little confidence and had poor communication skills. The challenge we took was to take ordinary students (academically average) and make them perform extraordinarily. This is a time-tested method that I have been experiencing for several years now.

This book can certainly help every young person to move a notch or two higher in life – if they want to.

Today, you live in New India or *Naya Bharat*. The world is looking up to us; the Western world is on the decline in whichever way you look at it. The government is determined to push the economy and has announced dozens of schemes for the youth. Start-up India is encouraging you to start your own business and generate employability. Be your own boss. New opportunities are coming up every day. The top leadership has set the ball rolling, and the climate is right for foreign investments in a big way. It is happening in India. At the time of writing, our FOREX is at an all-time high, crossing $600 billion. Do not lose this opportunity to make it big, and you can do it.

Let us dig into what other experts say. Don't mind the jargon.

Setting yourself apart from the rest. You got to be unique–first amongst equals

Be clear in your mind about your unique selling proposition (USP): It's also important to start thinking about what your USP is. While you've almost certainly heard of USPs, you've probably only ever associated them with the marketing of products or services rather than people. The principles of USPs can also apply to job seekers.

To realize your USP, you need to do a question-answer session with yourself.

- Why should an employer hire you over any other candidate?
- What is it that you can bring to the table that other candidates can't?
- What unique skills or experiences do you have that could add real value?
- Do you consider yourself to be particularly creative or innovative?
- With a backdrop of increasing automation, human skills such as creativity are set to become increasingly important to employers in the decades ahead. So, keep this in mind as you embark on your job search.
- Having a hobby shows initiative and a willingness to learn. It will also assist you in writing the 'hobbies' or 'interests' part of your résumé. One important spin-off is that this provides an opportunity to meet more people and gain varied perspectives.

You Got to Showcase Yourself

Maintain a portfolio of your prime work; whether it's a sample of your fiction writing, digital art or videos, it pays to maintain a portfolio of your prime work at college. Show off your hard work with a physical copy and/or ensure that you update it. Employers always prefer a candidate's portfolio, so it's worth setting up one. Portfolio aside, you could also keep a collection of all your work, both the good and the bad, to identify your strengths and weaknesses and the areas where you need to improve.

Also, it's important to think about any specific examples you can cite, which clearly evidence your USPs to both recruiters and hiring managers. Perhaps your innovative thinking and new ideas led to new processes being rolled out, and thus time and money were saved.

I remember selecting a candidate for an MBA program whose USP was that while doing his B.Com from a small town, he used to help his father with his business. They owned a few stone-crushing plants and a quarry. He was the only child of rich parents but still worked on the plants, and he knew the entire business model backwards.

This showed the panel that despite being the only child of rich parents, he didn't waste his time as most youngsters from affluent backgrounds do, and he also had that extra zing to do well in life. On top of that, he was polite, grounded and humble. After doing his MBA, he is doing very well in his profession.

Power skills is the new name for soft skills, and they 'don't relate to what work you do, but HOW you work, and the extra mile you are prepared to go,' explains Lisa Bodell, Founder of FutureThink, an award-winning accelerated learning company, in her impulse talk.

Current times no longer demand an 'I'-shaped person, someone with a lot of depth and knowledge (hard skills) on a specific job that you would be hired to do. Now, we are experiencing changes, and it is 'no longer just about hard skills, it's about the breadth of an individual', Lisa explained. A person with a combination of hard and power skills can be termed a 'T'-shaped person.

> *"Being a T shaped person sets you apart and gets you ahead. It's not enough anymore just to have great specific skills, it's your ability to leverage them between and beyond the business unit that you work in".*
>
> —Lisa Bodell

Today, it is 'jack of all and master of some'. People are looking for street-smart guys who can solve unexpected problems.

To illustrate an example of a 'T'-shaped person, Lisa referenced the scientists who have created the COVID-19 vaccines. She stated that the *I* part of them is the knowledge they have on vaccinology needed to create it, but the *T* part is what gave them the ability to work with teams from around the world, deal with the stress of such a task, and respond quickly and effectively to the virus. Lisa states, 'Power skills are what will set you apart and what will set organizations apart in the future. They're what make you different and what gets you promoted'.

Remember, for every job where a graduate applies, there are ten more guys in the lineup. So, you have to sell yourself.

Therefore, you need to expand your learning horizon. According to LinkedIn Learning, the most sought-after power skills are creativity, resilience, adaptability, leading through change, emotional intelligence, collaboration, time management, communication, dealing with stress and being mindful. Resilience and adaptability were deemed the most sought-after power skills that CEOs want to have on their teams.

Work on Holistic Learning

Students who take an interdisciplinary approach to learning are more prepared for the future world of work. It fosters curiosity while also improving communication and social skills.

Students are encouraged to make connections in a subject by using their creative skills, which will later assist them in engaging in industry-related activities.

There is, therefore, hope for those who have missed the boat or have now woken up to get hold of themselves to do well in life. This could be during the eleventh or twelfth class in school or during graduation or even during postgraduation or while doing a distance-learning program or once you are employed. You can "sharpen your axe" any time. The time is always right, provided you start.

> *"The best way to not feel hopeless is to get up and do something. Don't wait for good things to happen to you. If you go out and make some good things happen, you will fill the world with hope, you will fill yourself with hope".*
>
> —Barack Obama

Therefore, start now!

What is Your Success Quotient?

Before you read this book, answer the following questions honestly. Write yes or no in front of each question.

1. Are you inquisitive and keen to know and learn new things?
2. Do you have a sense of humour? Do you like cracking jokes?
3. Are you always punctual and value time?
4. Are you an organized person?
5. Do you have any hobbies?
6. Do you like reading newspapers regularly?
7. Do you play any musical instrument?
8. Do you like listening to music?
9. Do you make friends quickly?
10. Do you have more than six friends (not Facebook friends)?
11. Do people think that you are disciplined?
12. Do you sleep early? Before 11:30 PM?
13. Do you take interest in what job your father is doing to earn money?
14. Are you ambitious and want to do well in life?
15. Are you law-abiding and respect authority?
16. Do you break rules?
17. Are you helpful to others?
18. Are you emphatic to others?
19. Do you lose your temper quickly?
20. Do you like to dress up properly?

21. Do you participate in discussions with friends?
22. Do you like animals or pets?
23. Are you good at handling failure?
24. Can you handle criticism?
25. Do you respect your teachers?
26. Do you respect your parents and are courteous to them?
27. Do you help parents with jobs to be done at home or little jobs outside?
28. Do you think your friends like you?
29. Do you have any habits you are proud of?
30. Do you read books?
31. Do you watch movies?
32. Do you watch news channels every day or regularly to remain updated?
33. Do you keep yourself fit by regularly exercising?
34. Are you clear about what you want to achieve in life?
35. Are you diplomatic?
36. Do you feel you are hard-working?
37. Do you like to travel?
38. Do you usually make a backup plan?
39. Do you first complete a task before starting another?
40. Can you work under pressure?
41. You are NOT stubborn, are you?
42. Are you patriotic?
43. Are you a good mediator (can you resolve a conflict between two people)?
44. You are not too emotional or sensitive, are you?
45. Do you take criticism positively?
46. Do you admit a mistake and can apologize and take responsibility?
47. You do not blame others for your mistakes, do you?
48. Can you take failure in your stride?
49. Do you learn from your mistakes?
50. Do you handle personal finance properly?
51. Do you finish a task given to you on time (for example, a college project)?

52. Do you take initiative to do new things?
53. It does not take long for you to calm down when you've been angry, does it?
54. You are not easily disappointed, are you?
55. Are you considerate of other people's feelings?
56. You DO NOT feel overwhelmed often, do you?
57. Are you generally passionate about social causes?
58. 'I like to solve complex problems'. Yes or no?
59. 'I would never cheat on my taxes'. Yes or no?
60. 'I will not cheat anyone'. Yes or no?
61. 'I try to follow the rules'. Yes or no?
62. 'I warm up quickly to others'. Yes or no?
63. 'I try to lead others'. Yes or no?
64. 'I am a go-getter'. Yes or no?
65. 'I seek adventure'. Yes or no?
66. 'I feel others' emotions'. Yes or no?
67. 'I anticipate the needs of others'. Yes or no?
68. 'I feel sympathy and feel sorry for those who are worse off than me'. Yes or no?
69. 'I keep my promises'. Yes or no?
70. 'I am always prepared'. Yes or no?
71. 'I am proactive'. Yes or no?
72. 'I feel comfortable around people'. Yes or no?
73. 'I enjoy being part of a group'. Yes or no?
74. 'I have a rich vocabulary'. Yes or no?
75. 'I consider myself an average person'. Yes or no?
76. 'I value cooperation over competition'. Yes or no?
77. 'I always return a favour'. Yes or no?
78. 'I start a given task right away'. Yes or no?
79. 'I love action'. Yes or no?
80. 'I can convince others into doing things'. Yes or no?
81. 'I am not fearful of public speaking'. Yes or no?
82. 'I like dramatics'. Yes or no?
83. 'I hate wasting time'. Yes or no?
84. 'I want everything to be "just right"'. Yes or no?

85. 'I pay my bills on time'. Yes or no?
86. 'I turn plans into actions'. Yes or no?
87. 'I dislike procrastination'. Yes or no?
88. 'If I take up a job, I make sure I do my best to do it'. Yes or no?
89. 'I am positive in my approach'. Yes or no?
90. 'I am an optimist'. Yes or no?
91. 'I take charge of a situation'. Yes or no?
92. 'I feel I am a self-starter'. Yes or no?
93. 'I love excitement'. Yes or no?
94. 'I am not easily intimidated or cowed down'. Yes or no?
95. 'You respect the value of time'. Yes or no?
96. 'You know how to enjoy life'. Yes or no?
97. 'You know how to cheer up a friend or a teammate'. Yes or no?
98. 'I know how to build trust'. Yes or no?
99. 'I am aware of the value of trust'. Yes or no?
100. 'I am a conscientious person'. Yes or no?
101. 'I like to keep fit and take care of my health and diet'. Yes or no?

For every yes, give yourself one mark. Ignore the no.

Interpretation of Scores

- A score between 80 and 101 is a thumbs up for you. This reflects you can really do well in life. Take corrective action for questions where you got a no; there is always room for improvement. Don't become complacent.
- A score between 60 and 80 reflects that you have good potential, and with a little effort, you can do better. Look at where you didn't tick a yes, and work on these qualities to do better.
- A score below 60 reflects that you need to work hard on your attitude. Look where you have given a no for yourself and focus on these issues to make a change in your approach to life in general and work in particular.

Part 1: Path to a Successful Career

1
Why You Need a Mentor

"Mentoring is a brain to pick, an ear to listen, and a push in the right direction".

—John C. Crosby

It's immensely beneficial to have a friend, philosopher and guide all rolled into one. Such a person is called a mentor. A mentor would provide you with knowledge, the right ways to do things and guidance, which will open doors of success for you. It was Joe Weider, a Canadian bodybuilder and co-founder of the International Federation of Body Builders, who mentored Arnold Schwarzenegger. Mark Zuckerberg, who co-founded Facebook, had Marc Andreessen, founder of Netscape and Mosaic, as his mentor.

> *"Ninety-five per cent of mentoring participants said the experience motivated them to do their very best".*
>
> —The War for Talent

As per Forbes, employees who received mentoring were promoted five times more often than people who didn't have mentors.[1] Therefore, mentoring is not just a great idea but a proven concept that has worked over the years. Let's get you on the path of finding a mentor now!

A Mentor for You

Our parents usually ask us to work hard, take tuition, attend all classes and score higher marks. However, we find

1 Lisa Quast, "How Becoming A Mentor Can Boost Your Career," Forbes, October 31, 2011, https://www.forbes.com/sites/lisaquast/2011/10/31/how-becoming-a-mentor-can-boost-your-career/?sh=47772b835f57.

many intelligent and hardworking people not reaching their full potential in our surroundings. There is no one to tell them how to enhance their skills, utilize their time constructively and so forth. Parents, uncles and aunts may or may not have the knowledge, the know-how and sometimes not even the inclination to be able to guide you correctly.

But what if there was someone who identified their passion and encouraged them to make it a viable profession? Someone who inspired them to read more books, become confident, groom themselves and showed them the importance of emotional intelligence for an individual's success.

Let us face it: Education builds a foundation; it loads you with domain knowledge. For instance, if you are studying commerce, you will learn commerce; if you are doing a BA in English Literature, the course should make you sound in that subject or domain. But that is not sufficient in our context today. We need to do much more on our own to make the cut. That is the difference between successful and unsuccessful. Whosoever walks that extra mile will be the winner in the end.

Information Explosion

We are swamped by so much information that we are unable to decipher the relevant content out of this clutter. We need information that is useful to us, helps us to do better in life and helps us make the right choices in our personal life and career. We have a sea full of information, yet I find the young generation struggling.

There are magazines, portals, websites and online guides that, instead of giving a clear-cut direction, many times confuse us. Discussion boards and discussion sites often create clutter, and it is like one blind man guiding another blind man! For example, a mentor would guide you on choosing the right business school or give you tips on cracking tough interviews.

How to Choose the Right B-school?

Everyone cannot crack the top twenty B-schools, as they have a limited capacity. Even if, on average, a college has two thousand vacancies, twenty colleges make up just four thousand vacancies. There are a plethora of other colleges that are not ranked. Many of them are very good. Choosing the right one is a matter of a better understanding of what a college is equipped with, which matters the most.

A Mentor Would Ask Why You Want to Go to B-school

If your answer is 'to seek employment' or 'to get employment', you are on the wrong premises. You go to a B-school to 'become employable'.

Let's look at art and craft discipline; students who want to learn filmmaking and acting join institutes like FTII (Film and Television Institute of India) to learn the craft, not instantly get a break in Bollywood. They want to become more talented and skilled to enter the film industry with confidence, skills and talent. Similarly, a student looking at a professional program in this manner will most likely choose the right B-school.

Let us look at a few required parameters to benchmark a college. Please remember, when you want to buy a motorbike for yourself, you check so many brands, test ride all of them, check from friends who have this bike and verify it with customer feedback. You do the same while booking a hotel room. Selecting a college is more complicated than buying a motorbike or toothpaste. Remember, you don't do an MBA twice in life.

You, therefore, can't follow your instinct or go according to a hunch. You should not be impressed by advertisements on TV or in magazines and newspapers either. These could be misleading as well. Let us consider some basics.

(a) Brand names sometimes are misleading. It is unnecessary that a known brand—which could result from a massive branding exercise costing millions to the college—is a good college.

(b) A massive campus means little. Yes, a reasonably good campus, well-equipped classrooms, a play area and a library are required. Anything more than this is frivolous. Therefore, don't be impressed by the big campus, sports facilities and cafeterias alone. London School of Economics, one of the best colleges in the world, is on a less-than-five-acre campus. It has produced more than a dozen Nobel laureates. Therefore, a college boasting of a fifty-acre campus should not impress you.

(c) Teaching and curriculum are the backbone of education. You must look at the curriculum first. Try to understand how many subjects are taught across the entire course. In the case of B-schools, engineering or other professional courses, industry interface matters a lot. For B-schools especially, if there is a healthy mix of pure academicians and those from industry backgrounds, you can be sure of learning good content.

(d) How rigorous is the schedule? Most top B-schools and engineering colleges like IITs have a very tough schedule. The classes could be six to eight hours a day, but assignments, student activities, competitions and preparations for next-day class take up a lot of time. Usually, the first year is so rigorous that students are continuously engaged with schoolwork. The same is true for top B-schools such as IIMs, Symbiosis and XLRI. While some colleges have a leisurely schedule, and it may be a cozy arrangement for some, it ultimately builds students' complacency. The goal of an institution is to put students through the academic and college-based grind that justifies college tuition so that they can compete in the real world. Please remember that engaging the students requires effort from the college management and costs them money. So let the college work hard on you.

(e) Industry internship is the most critical part of learning. Whether in a graduation course or a PG course, an internship changes the personality and perspective of a student. The degree of seriousness is no less, and being responsive and responsible is inescapable. Here, practical learning, dealing with people and contributing to the organization is a mandatory part of the job. It is observed that students who return from summer projects are more confident, wiser and ready to enter the job market with more vigor than before. You must opt for a college that is serious about summer placements and ensures that every student gets an adequately structured project.

> *"If you feel your school is failing you, the question is why. Is it a lack of parental involvement, large classes, school violence, poor learning environment? Are there any standards to determine where problems are? Are there tutoring or mentoring programs? If the school is still failing after 3 years then what are your options"?*
>
> —John Rowland

This information would have undoubtedly helped any B-school aspirant. Most of them would not have known these intricacies of an educational institute. Hence, having a mentor or reading a mentor's work is the way to grow in life.

Cracking a Job interview

After graduation, every student wants to apply for a job. Some want to pursue postgraduate studies, but most are happy to get a job first. My experience tells me that students are often ill-prepared for a job. They don't know what to say during an interview and go there based on the degree that they have in hand. This never works.

In his opening address, Prime Minister Narendra Modi, on the floor of the Lok Sabha, said something very important and proper. He retold a story of a graduate who was interviewed for a job and asked, 'Aaap kya kar sakte hain [What can you do?]'? The boy answered, 'Sir, I am a graduate.' He was again asked the same question, and he replied, 'I am a graduate'. The interviewer said, 'I know you are a graduate, but what can you do'? The answer for the fourth time was, 'Sir, I am a graduate'. As a result, he did not get the job.

The aforementioned example tells us that a graduation degree could give you some domain knowledge but does not make you employable. Here's what I can share from my experience of interviewing thousands of graduates of all shades and grades.

In an interview, what a potential employer is looking for is your capacity to comprehend information and use your intellect to complete tasks. That means your attitude towards life and work comes first. Second, you should be familiar with the basics of the subjects you studied for your graduation. Third, what extra work have you done besides your graduation (the most crucial differentiator!)?

1. Your attitude

As a graduate, you must understand that you are not being interviewed for the CEO or managing director position of a company. No one is expecting something great from you and asking you to make a strategy or financial plan for the company. You will be working under some experienced executives who will be there to supervise your work and guide you. At least in the initial period, there will be a lot of hand-holding. The interviewers are looking for a person who is willing to work, has a pleasant personality and is willing to learn and give their best to the organization. Good communication skills, a decent turnout and a display of enthusiasm is best. There are several soft skills books and coaching classes available online or offline. Go for them!

2. Knowledge of subject matter

Basic domain knowledge is something that you cannot do without. Nothing is more annoying for an interview panel than a candidate falling short on this. As a commerce graduate, you must know the basics of commerce. If you are an economics graduate, you must have adequate subject knowledge. The same goes for an engineer. Most of the time, candidates pay too much attention to dressing sense and communication skills but fail to read what they studied in graduation before going for an interview. In addition, you must be thorough with the internship project you did during graduation. Not knowing about it is a cardinal sin! The upside is that if you have done your project sincerely, you are a winner because you know more about your project than the interviewer! In fact, get the interview panel to ask you questions regarding your project. You are getting them on your home ground.

3. That extra mile

'What is that something extra that you did?' This is the key to finally cracking an interview. Did you participate in any college activity or were in charge of a student committee? Did you design a T-shirt for a college fest or organize a ramp show, a college orchestra or a blood-donation camp? Did you work with an NGO alone or help your dad in his business alongside your studies? Do you read books, write for the college journal or play in a sport? All these matters a lot. A course in a foreign language, graffiti, calligraphy or handwriting analysis? This extra mile tells the interviewer that you are inclined to do more work than prescribed or assigned to you. I have seen many students getting a job on the basis of what they did over and above the curriculum. This book will focus primarily on this extra mile, which I call the 'zing factor'.

> *"The delicate balance of mentoring someone is not creating them in your own image, but giving them the opportunity to create themselves".*
>
> —Steven Spielberg

Where the road to success is long and tardy, you will be able to go through it. To bring out the potential in you, you need a guide or a mentor who can hold your hand and tell you what to do step by step. This book will do just that.

2

You are Living in the Age of Opportunities, Options and Possibilities

"A dream doesn't become reality through magic; it takes sweat, determination and hard work".

—Colin Powell

Just a decade ago, people were excited about the information age and digital era. Worldwide digital connectivity coupled with optimized mass production of goods has changed the way business is done and the way money can be generated. Much more has been achieved by our civilization in the last fifty years than what was achieved in the last thousand years.

All this is possible only if you can pay for all this when you are capable of earning money. According to an article in Global Issues, around three billion people in the world live on less than \$2.5 a day (₹165), which is less than ₹5,000 a month.[1] In India, the report says 30 per cent of the population (i.e., 375 crores) live below \$1.9 a day (₹125), which is around ₹3,750 a month.[2]

Despite the decline in extreme poverty, broader measures show that billions still struggle to meet basic needs.

1. "Poverty Facts and Stats," January 7, 2013, https://www.globalissues.org/article/26/poverty-facts-and-stats.
2. Pti, "India Has Highest Number of People Living below Poverty Line: World Bank," *Business Today*, October 3, 2016, https://www.businesstoday.in/latest/economy-politics/story/india-has-highest-number-of-people-living-below-poverty-line-world-bank-69179-2016-10-03.

The World Bank estimates that around 8.5 per cent of the world's population (685 million people) could be extremely poor by the end of 2022 and that poverty is now declining at a very slow rate of only 2 per cent a year.[3]

Living on less than $3.20 per day reflects poverty lines in lower-middle-income countries, while $5.50 a day reflects standards in upper-middle-income countries, the World Bank said in its biennial Poverty and Shared Prosperity Report, 'Piecing Together the Poverty Puzzle'.[4]

The silver lining to this dark cloud is that there are a lot of opportunities in India to make a good living. This needs a focused approach, appropriate mentoring and hard work.

Today, well-paying jobs, business opportunities and creative options are restricted only by your imagination. You name it, and you can have it. Those who are smart enough, willing to work hard and demonstrate a quick learning curve would be able to get maximum bang for the buck. Today, people are ready to back great ideas and pay for hard work and deliverables. Are you ready for it?

> *"The evolving social and digital media platforms and highly innovative and relevant payment capabilities are causing seismic changes in consumer behavior and creating equally disruptive opportunities for business".*
>
> —Howard Schultz

Shortage of Manpower

Survey[5] after survey shows that our industry is facing a shortage of people, more so at entry-level jobs—the banking sector, manufacturing, real estate, aviation, hospitality, pharmaceutical industry, media, marketing, tourism,

3. "The Forgotten 3 Billion | Brookings," Brookings, October 25, 2022, https://www.brookings.edu/blog/future-development/2022/10/21/the-forgotten-3-billion/.
4. World bank, "Piecing Together the Poverty Puzzle," *Worldbank.Org*, 2018, https://openknowledge.worldbank.org/server/api/core/bitstreams/34b63a7c-7c89-5474-b9d3-f4f35085fe83/content.
5. "Hiring Challenges In The FMCG Sector Explained," n.d.; Crossley, "Shortage of Workers Main Challenge for FMCG Sector: Godrej."; "People Matters - Interstitial Site — People Matters."

entertainment, FMCG industry, textile, consulting, IT, telecom, ITES, energy, automobile industry, education, agriculture sector and so on; the list is huge. This is an immense opportunity which you cannot afford to miss. You can make the best of it if you prepare for it.

Don't ask for *haq* (right); become *haquedar* (worthy). Don't take things as your right, but work towards becoming deserving. There is a big difference between the two. Remember, no government can generate jobs, but they may be able to create a good environment. So, when a politician says, 'We will create these many jobs if you vote for us', then ask him, 'How do you plan to do this'? You will get your answer.

Be Your Own Boss

The most capable, ambitious and hardworking will not seek jobs as another new opportunity awaits them. They can start their own business and become entrepreneurs. They will generate employment for others. The government is backing up such young minds. There are schemes to fund such ideas by the government and angel investors. As your business grows and becomes profitable, you will have offers from venture capital companies and private equity funds to take your net worth manifold. Instead of job seekers, you will become job givers.

America is a nation of entrepreneurs, and its economy was primarily created by individuals who had big dreams! Three greats of the twentieth century were Henry Ford, Alexander Graham Bell and J. D. Rockefeller. They had dreams and worked very hard to reach their exalted destination. These gentlemen were there when America was on the cusp of taking a giant leap. America leapt forward, and so did they.

India is standing at that cusp today—ready to leap forward—and you, the young Indians, have the same opportunity that Ford, Bell and Rockefeller had in those days. You have a chance to leap forward!!

Let Us Dig a Bit Into History

Henry Ford created the Ford Motor Company, and much after his death, his net worth was estimated at $199 billion in

2013.[6] Alexander Graham Bell created Bell Labs, a mammoth company that won eight Nobel Prize awards. It later became AT&T Bell Labs and recently is called Nokia Bell Labs. J. D. Rockefeller, an American oil industrialist, is called the wealthiest American of all time, with a net worth of $392 billion in 2016. He later built several institutions and universities of repute.

The spirit of entrepreneurship is still intact, and we see the modern billionaires of America in Bill Gates, who created Microsoft; Mark Zuckerberg, founder of Facebook; and Steve Jobs, the co-founder and CEO of Apple Inc. Though the wealth-generating methodology has changed from a smoke-stacked industrial economy to an ITES and service-based economy, the spirit and enthusiasm to be your master remain the same.

America boasts of companies that are trillion dollars worth—many small nations don't have this kind of money.[7] The following gives you some idea; these figures keep changing as per market conditions but are good\ enough to understand the point.

Company	Market Capitalization
Microsoft Corporation	$2.51 trillion
Alphabet Inc	$1.97 trillion
Amazon.com Inc	$1.79 trillion
Tesla Inc	$1.07 trillion

Source: Reuters[8]

The American economy, entrepreneurship and affluence were supported to the hilt by the US government from the very beginning.

6. "How Henry Ford Became Rich | Melbado," n.d., https://melbado.com/how-henry-ford-became-rich/.
7. ZeeBiz WebDesk, "Google Parent Company Alphabet Eyes Elite $2 Trillion Market Valuation after Blowout Results," *Zee Business*, February 3, 2022, https://www.zeebiz.com/world/news-google-parent-company-alphabet-eyes-elite-2-trillion-market-valuation-after-blowout-results-177971.
8. Reuters, "Factbox: Tech Giants Dominate Wall Street's Trillion-Dollar Club," *Reuters*, December 9, 2021, https://www.reuters.com/markets/europe/tech-giants-dominate-wall-streets-trillion-dollar-club-2021-12-09.

> *"The road to success is not easy to navigate, but with hard work, drive and passion, it's possible to achieve the American dream".*
>
> —Tommy Hilfiger

For instance, the US government sanctioned the Panama Canal project to connect the Atlantic Ocean to the Pacific. This lasted for ten years, from 1904–14. Millions of jobs were generated while building this 77 km long canal over ten years. To date, more than 815,000 vessels have passed through this canal, which halved the distance to transport goods from America's East Coast to the West Coast.

After the Second World War, Americans under the Marshall Plan started reconstructing Europe. It was a massive opportunity for the Americans to generate wealth and employment. A significant portion of the investment was also used to import American-made goods and food. American government spent $13 billion, and the return was equivalent to $98 billion by 2011.

From 1954 to 1991, thirty-five years was dedicated to building a vast interstate highway system. President Dwight D. Eisenhower perceived and envisioned this as an opportunity to connect America. In all, fifty American states were involved. It generated wealth, jobs and prosperity for the American people. The government invested $125 billion and, in return, got $468 billion by 2011. It created 42,795 centerline miles of road, connecting the largest economy in the world. In all, sixteen billion tons of freight worth $15 trillion moved across the nation's highways in 2011.

A dream of President John F. Kennedy—the Apollo space program—catapulted the American people into a long-range exploration of space. With twenty thousand partnering institutes, it employed four hundred thousand Americans. A mere $24 billion turned into $150 billion in 2011. It also helped make America a superpower.

Thousands of entrepreneurs in America, Europe and the rest of the world generated huge wealth for themselves and created millions of jobs. India is now a hotbed of entrepreneurs and big business houses. Tatas, Birlas and Ambanis were the ones who made a mark a little earlier. They were followed by Azim Premji of Wipro, Narayan Murthi of Infosys and Shiv Nadar of HCL Technologies. Now, we see Flipkart, Paytm, Snapdeal, OYO Rooms, Vista Rooms, Ola and many more doing great business.

"If you are faced with a mountain, you have several options.

You can climb it and cross to the other side.

You can go around it.

You can dig under it.

You can fly over it.

You can blow it up.

You can ignore it and pretend it's not there.

You can turn around and go back the way you came.

Or you can stay on the mountain and make it your home".

—Vera Nazarian

India is the Right Destination for the World

Today, India's political scenario is vibrant, and the government is trying to bootstrap the economy. It is doing all that can be done to push the GDP upwards and generate jobs. It is trying to create a conducive financial and ecosystem governance for entrepreneurial growth. Digital India is a reality today. The state is investing in infrastructure, roads and highways, railways, energy, biotechnology, textiles, pharma, tourism, agriculture, defence and manufacturing, to name a few. When the government invests, the nation moves and people benefit.

You need not be an Albert Einstein to move forward and make a kill.

Jobs or own business, the sky is the limit. The fruits are hanging low, but you need to jump and pluck them; they will not fall in your lap without effort.

New entrants to the workforce must take the responsibility of being employable themselves. Companies are looking for young, passionate, hardworking graduates to fill junior positions, and only the most employable graduates will be offered these career-starting opportunities. On the other hand, young men and women who want to become entrepreneurs must also sharpen their axe. This space is cluttered, and only smart, well-informed, hardworking people will survive. You need to smarten up and become ready to face the competitive world.

You cannot be educated and earn money; you must be 'skeducated'. Skeducation is skill-based education that needs to make people employable. Unfortunately, they don't teach you this in universities. You have got to do it yourself. Are you ready?

> *"Nothing depends on luck; everything depends on work because even luck has to work".*
>
> —Bhagavad Gita

Are you any less? Would you not like a share of the pie?

3
Learn and Know

"The best education happens outside the classroom".

—Mark Twain

We spend three to four years in college, blaming the system and our fortune, but take no active steps for our own progress. And you know what comes out of college finally? A youth with a lot of potential but no more experienced than the child who entered college.

This chapter will guide you in actively creating your own learning path during your college years. Just a change in your attitude and approach to life is enough! Let me assure you that even if you change 40 percent in your attitude and follow some of these things, you will be able to transform yourself to a great extent.

> *"Reading is to the mind what exercise is to the body".*
>
> —Richard Steele

Tackling Distractions and Enabling Meaningful Learning

Gadgets such as TV, radio, the internet, Facebook, Twitter and WhatsApp, to name a few constantly bombarded us with so much data in bits and pieces that our mind is unable to meaningfully absorb all that. These sources give us information but seldom help augment our vocabulary, expression and writing style.

You would relate that during the exams, we know the answer but cannot put it across appropriately. Many times, we cannot put forth the right word at the right place. We have everything in our heads and yet fail to use the perfect expression to explain our point. This is called articulation. Like Mark Twain rightly said, 'The difference between the almost right word and the right word is really a large matter—'tis the difference between the lightning bug and the lightning'.

Reading books and articles in magazines provides us with an alternative to get a better command over the language and express ourselves better. Every author has a writing style, and reading different authors on different subjects can enrich our ability to communicate effectively. It is also important to read books on different topics and varied genres. For example, fiction, biography, thrillers, mystery and drama can all add to our knowledge and take us to varying levels of intellectual prowess.

Always keep in mind and remember that you studied from textbooks in schools and colleges for more than twenty years of your life, and whatever knowledge you gained, learnt and retained was through books and therefore you cannot ignore the power of reading and the ability to learn from books and reading material.

Organic Learning

Reading books is learning the natural way, whereas e-learning is electronic learning. Learning, reading and writing are basic cognitive skills, and the human brain has a way of absorbing and retaining information, data and knowledge. Reading and writing is an organic learning methodology.

Compelling reasons why books are better than videos

- Books are meant to be read in short spurts, bit by bit. You can put it down while you get a snack or a drink and think about what you just read, and then pick it up again, re-read and so on. That is why you have bookmarks, not 'video marks' per se. You have to think about, interact with and imagine the material. Video is just a one-way street where you are rushing in a high-speed car that is meant to be digested and swallowed quickly without much time to think critically, reflect on or process. If you go as a visitor to a foreign land or even a different town, the tourist bus can whizz past all crucial points, but you always want to spend time at each spot; that is how our brains work. For instance, if you go to Paris, you would like to walk down the shopping streets looking at every shop, inadvertently absorbing each detail at your own leisurely pace.

- Reading a book is more gripping than watching a film based on the same story. One primary reason is that a book allows you to imagine according to your imagination, whereas a movie is the director's interpretation. For instance, walking through a dark, scary street can be shown in one way in a movie, but you can imagine it in a dozen different ways.
- Videos are usually disjointed pieces of debris floating through cyberspace. This format feeds and confuses your mind, that part of your brain that swings from idea to idea with no pattern or discipline, like a monkey going across trees in a Tarzan movie.[1] Conversely, a book is a format that focuses your mind on a single topic for a reasonable amount of time.
- Video is processed by a human brain sixty thousand times faster than text, says Psychology Today.[2] It bypasses your cognitive mind and drives straight to your emotions, encouraging lazy thinking. Reading, on the other hand, is interactive and more absorbing. You have to form mental pictures and focus on translating shapes on a page into ideas in your mind. This medium makes you a robust, more disciplined thinker regardless of what you read.

---

1. Yussuf, "Reading vs Watching Videos: What Science Says - Digital Minimalism," Digital Minimalism, April 27, 2022, https://digitalminimalism.com/reading-vs-watching-videos-what-science-says/.
2. Yussuf, "Reading vs Watching Videos: What Science Says - Digital Minimalism."

Where to Begin?

Initially, one must start reading simple, short books on topics that attract you. This will help you get into a habit of reading without putting you off. As you go along and develop a liking, you can try your hand at little more complex topics. It is not a bad idea to start with comics and short stories, as they are very interesting and can be finished in a short span of time.

> *"I find television very educating. Every time somebody turns on the set, I go into the other room and read a book".*
>
> —Groucho Marx

Great People Read a Lot

Mahatma Gandhi, Dr. Abdul Kalam and Nehru read many books, and they were influenced by authors like Leo Tolstoy, Charles Dickens and many more.

US president Barrack Obama says that books played an indispensable role during his presidency and throughout his life. 'At a time when events move so quickly and so much information is transmitted', he said, reading gave him the ability to occasionally 'slow down and get perspective' and 'the ability to get in somebody else's shoes'.[3] President Roosevelt read two books a day and John F. Kennedy, who had a phenomenal reading speed, was also a voracious reader.

An avid reader, JFK could read approximately 1,200 words per minute, nearly ten times the average. In fact, he would reportedly read six newspapers every morning at breakfast, cover to cover. He groomed his reading skills throughout his life. As a boy, due to constant illness, he was constantly stuck in hospital beds; almost by divine providence, books became his escape from such gloomy circumstances.[4]

---

3. Michiko Kakutani, "Obama's Secret to Surviving the White House Years: Books," *The New York Times*, September 17, 2020, https://www.nytimes.com/2017/01/16/books/obamas-secret-to-surviving-the-white-house-years-books.html.
4. Wikipedia contributors. "Speed Reading." Wikipedia, October 16, 2023. https://en.wikipedia.org/wiki/Speed_reading#:~:text=Kennedy%20was%20a%20proponent%20of,of%201%2C200%20words%20per%20minute.

Ms. Jackie Kennedy said, “Well, he read in the strangest way. I mean, I could never read unless I’d have a rainy afternoon or a long evening in bed, or something. He’d read walking; he’d read at the table, at meals; he’d read after dinner; he’d read in the bathtub; he’d read – prop open a book on his desk – on his bureau, while he was doing his tie”.[5]

Before they got married, Jackie says he used to give her books to read. One of his favourites that he especially urged her to finish was Pilgrim’s Way by John Buchan; anyone he hoped to understand him would urge him to read this book. He was an intellectual motivator in a way.

Another book he read as a child was Marlborough by Winston Churchill. The book is a biography of Churchill’s best-known ancestor, John Churchill, the first Duke of Marlborough. I suppose, at this point, Winston has managed the upper hand with the family name.

The Prime Minister of Great Britain, Winston Churchill, had read hundreds of books. Abraham Lincoln, who could not get too much formal education, made it up by reading books and was self-educated. Many CEOs and senior executives in the corporate world read a lot.

Prashant, one of my friends who studied in a vernacular medium till school, did his engineering, went to IIM Ahmedabad, worked for an MNC, and now speaks and writes perfect English. He says that reading books gave him all the success and confidence.

Build Your Road to Success

Make it a habit to visit the best bookshops and libraries and buy books for yourself. Build a small personal library and be proud of it. Your parents will never say no to this. Read newspapers and magazines which are available very easily. Excellent second-hand books are available at a throwaway price, which can cut your budget drastically. Online portals

5. Jj, “Camelot: Once There Was a Spot: A Love of Words~ J.Jones,” Camelot: One Brief Shining Moment, February 24, 2021, https://pastprettie.wordpress.com/2021/02/24/camelot-once-there-was-a-spot-a-love-of-words-j-jones/.

also give a good discount, and one can look at millions of books sitting at home.

The busiest and most successful people read, read and read.

Warren Buffett reads five hundred pages a day.

Mark Cuban reads three hours a day.

Bill Gates Reads Fifty Books a Year

Successful people are selective about what they read, electing to read educational books and publications over entertaining literature. They also tend to fixate on reading about other successful people and their stories.

Elon Musk taught himself to build rockets by reading. The costs to build a rocket were prohibitively high, so Musk concluded he could do it himself after reading how to do it. He was driven by a specific goal and a desire to acquire specific knowledge. He didn't stop until he learnt what he wanted to learn.

Perhaps the successes of others are enough to jump-start your lifelong reading habit. Happy reading!

Bollywood Bookworms

Shah Rukh Khan is a book hoarder. In an old interview, he even said, 'I read anything and everything. . .I read three or four books at a time. I go to bookstores when I'm in London or America. I get a coffee and keep browsing for hours—something I can't do in India'.[6]

Saif Ali Khan is also a book reader like his sister. Just like his sister, on many occasions, Saif is seen reading a book at his place. He even has a personal library at home, which shows how much he loves reading.

Twinkle Khanna, too, is an avid reader. After her acting career, she turned herself into a successful author. She is not only a bestselling author but also an avid reader. Knowing the importance of reading, she has also incorporated the habits into her kids.

---

6. Neelima Chimnani, "| Femina.In," *Femina*, April 23, 2020, https://www.femina.in/gossip/celeb-buzz/inside-srks-library-4520.html.

What Books to Read? Don't Get Stuck With One Genre

You must read different authors because every author has a writing style, and you get to learn different expressions from different authors.

If you don't read, you will not be able to write. This is important not only for the first job but also as you move up the promotion ladder.

Read Different Genres

You must read racy novels, thrillers, mysteries, autobiographies/biographies of great people, history and classics; the list could be endless.

> *"A reader lives a thousand lives before he dies. . .The man who never reads lives only one".*
>
> —George R.R. Martin

Read Magazines

It would be best if you should read for fun, too—anything you are fond of, such as gossip, health, automobiles, travel or even food. You should not be serious all the time. All these magazines give you a lot of information and help build a better grip on the language.

But to build intellect and core knowledge, read India Today, CSR, Manorama Yearbook, The Week and Businessworld. Read newspapers you like; read the Edit Page main articles; they give a great perspective on current affairs.

Hobbies Are the Biggest Learning Opportunities

Hobbies are a reflection of your attitude. A+T+T+I+T+U+D+E = 100 if you take the alphabet from A=1 to Z = 26. Fortune is 99. Try it.

Interview Tip: Cultivate a hobby for enjoyment and also employment that adds weight to your résumé.

From the job perspective, the interviewers basically look for an extra spark, something more than the usual people do. If ten people are applying for a job and, let us say, all have a similar or identical CV and educational competence, a person with a great hobby has a better chance of cracking the interview and getting the job. Remember, a job interviewer hiring a fresher is not looking for an Einstein or a perfect job fit. He is looking for a candidate who can walk the extra mile, is willing to learn and has a hobby that gives away that the boy has taken the initiative besides his studies and has picked up something else, too. It reflects a positive go-getter attitude. It reflects that you are a keen learner. You are trainable, and the company will train you for a specific role. Remember, attitude is more important than anything.

In colleges, there are hobby clubs for debating, music, social service, Student Government and Political Clubs, outdoor clubs, dramatics, and so on. I learned how to play the guitar and the drums during my college days. MP Shashi Tharoor graduated with a Bachelor of Arts in history from St Stephen's College, University of Delhi, where he had been president of the student union and founded the St Stephen's Quiz Club. He was a sought-after debater, too. He carries that to his image and advantage to date.

Hobbies Can Become Roaring Business Success

> *"The finest thing about a hobby is that you can't do any pretending about it. You either like it or you don't".*
>
> —Dorothy Draper

In the United States, a large number of people became entrepreneurs, converting hobbies into a business. When Mark Zuckerberg started a small social media website for students at Harvard University, it was just a hobby. It was more like a dating app or just fun—'who looks better'—and named it FaceMash. This prank-like stuff ultimately became Facebook—and blossomed into a multibillion-dollar global company. Today, his net worth is estimated to be just over $70 billion.

'I may have learned better coding and programming from small projects that I did than the courses in college', Zuckerberg said during a town hall event organized by North Carolina Agricultural and Technical State University.[7]

7. Zoë Miller, "14 People Who Turned Their Hobbies into Million- and Billion-Dollar Careers," *Insider*, November 15, 2018, https://www.insider.com/million-dollar-hobbies-careers-2018-6#mark-zuckerberg-facebook-6.

Harley-Davidson—Is it the world's most popular and sought-after motorcycle brand? This omnipresent motor vehicle began as the hobby of two friends, Arthur Davidson and William Harley, who saw the advent of the gasoline engine as a way to innovate bicycle design. Today, it is one of the biggest public companies in America.

Michael J. Kittredge made a candle of melted red crayons for his mother as a Christmas gift. He was sixteen years old then. He started making candles in his parent's garage and selling them at his school and to local businesses in his hometown. Kittredge was paying $80 a month by 1972 to rent a former paper mill as a workshop. Over a period, the primarily wholesale business had $1 billion in annual sales. Many years later, he took a loan to open a retail outlet and factory complex. By the mid-1990s, Yankee Candle had become very popular and a household name. Since they are built to last long and always have a high-performing wick, the Yankee Candle is an excellent choice for many people. Yankee Candles burn down evenly, taking a very long time to use up. The Yankee Candles are made of natural material, and therefore, they burn at a slower rate. Yankee Candle was sold for $1.75 billion to a consumer-product company, Jarden, in 2013.

Referring to her middle-class upbringing, Debbie Fields of Mrs. Fields said, 'My father believed that true wealth was found in family, friends and doing what you love.' For Fields, baking—cookies in particular—brought her joy. Even when her family couldn't afford real ingredients, she crafted cookies from margarine and imitation chocolate. Her famous chocolate chip cookie recipe launched a dessert empire worth hundreds of millions of dollars in time.

Importance of Short Certification Courses

Walk that extra mile, and you can sharpen the axe. You are lucky that today, there is no dearth of courses and teachers to teach you. Just to share one of the greatest success stories of modern times, which all started with one additional course that the founder of Apple computers, Steve Jobs, opted for after quitting college. Jobs attended Reed College in 1972 before withdrawing that same year and travelled through India in 1974, seeking enlightenment and studying Zen Buddhism (another out-of-the-box learning experience).

After he dropped out of college because the fee was too high for his parents to afford, Steve Jobs took a calligraphy class at Reed College based on the campus posters he saw. The poster fonts were artistic enough to catch his eye, and he joined this class. He and Wozniak co-founded Apple in 1976 to sell Wozniak's Apple I personal computer. Together, the duo gained fame and wealth a year later with the Apple II, one of the first highly successful mass-produced microcomputers. Steve was certainly hooked on the creativity of calligraphy. However, the classed instilled additional creative foundational elements in his mind that many business owners can use to reshape their brand and compete at a higher level.

Jobs was the first to give us a real choice of fonts and thus the ability to express ourselves digitally with emotion, clarity and variety. He made Type Gods of us all. He realized their value like no one else engaged in personal computers in the early 1980s, and suddenly, we were no longer dependent on professional printers or graphic designers.[8] Today, designers and marketers alike have nearly unlimited fonts and creative user interfaces for our digital devices. In a world dominated by ones and zeros, we all owe Jobs a debt of gratitude for bringing creativity into the world of technology.

Let me caution you. Do not link every certification course or learning with getting a job. Do certain things just because you want to do them or want to explore. Remember, Steve Jobs did a calligraphy course just for the heck of it, which made him do wonders in his business and innovation later. Any extra activity you do outside your college syllabus is a plus point, you never know when it will help you.

> *"Traveling—it leaves you speechless, then turns you into a storyteller".*
>
> —Ibn Battuta

8. Simon Garfield and Special To Cnn, "One Thing We Owe to Steve Jobs," *CNN*, October 6, 2011, https://edition.cnn.com/2011/10/05/opinion/garfield-steve-jobs-fonts/index.html.

Travelling is a Great Learning Experience

Travelling is something which quietly teaches you a lot. Here are a few reasons to travel and explore. You need not travel abroad alone; our own country is so vast and diverse that one can see a lot of new things and experience food as well as culture. Here are a few things that you can learn:

- You learn to plan. Which places to visit, how to manage travel and stay in your budget, book hotels and flights or train journey. Explore how to plan a backpacker's shoestring travel budget.
- Hones your communication skills. It helps you open up with people from different areas who speak different languages and have different attitudes.
- Adaptability is an essential thing. Getting used to different environments and managing them well is a quality not easy to learn in a classroom. Many students have never moved out of their towns or their comfort zones.
- Makes you self-reliant. You do not have your parents to help, and you need to handle tricky or sticky situations and people on your own.
- Widens your perspective and learning horizon. The more you travel, the more natural this becomes. When you're open to new perspectives, you'll be a better team player. You will be able to handle criticism more positively, which is crucial for your growth in the team. Also, travelling can open up your mind to bigger possibilities in life.
- Builds self-confidence. Travelling and doing things on your own builds a lot of confidence, and you can face up to anything and anyone for a chat.
- Gateway for new avenues. People have become authors, photographers, bloggers and even travel guides because of travelling. I know people who started a travel agency or an adventure camp as a spin-off.
- You learn to tell your experiences.

Teaching Others is the Biggest Learning

Now, this is extremely important, and very few venture into this. I know of a student who used to teach in school to earn some extra money. Later, she started coaching Air Force personnel in communication skills in Gwalior. She says that it was a great learning and confidence-building experience. At eighteen years of age, if you face up to forty men in uniform, it become a serious affair, and she had to work hard to prepare for her next class. This was one major reason for her getting selected for an MBA program. She did very well and contributed a lot to the college, too. Today, I am proud to say that she is doing very well professionally and is a senior HR manager in a big telecom company and is entirely responsible for campus recruitment!

Therefore, take tuition in any of the subjects you are good at. Volunteer to teach free of cost in schools in villages or small towns. Teach your friends free of cost. BYJUS'S is the story of Raveendran Byju, who started helping his friends crack competitive exams, and today he has become a billionaire. A big brand. From a small town, he did his engineering at the Government College of Engineering, Kannur, and not any IIT or US university. Raveendran went from teaching a few friends to teaching hundreds of students in large auditoriums and taking classes through satellite communication. Rest, as they say, is history.

> *"Taking initiative is a form of self-empowerment".*
>
> —Stephen R. Covey

Observe–observe–observe and Learn on the Go

Let me give you an example. At Symbiosis, as a director of a management institute, I started a student quiz program called the 'Telecom Grand Master' quiz. It had a lot of emphasis on marketing and products, and I kept it a broad-based quiz. I conceptualized it as a business quiz.

Year-on-year results surprised us. Students from non-telecom backgrounds did better! They could identify logos and products and hosts of other related things to business and marketing better than telecom guys. Our conclusion was that these guys were observant. They walked on the streets with their eyes open and their brain fully functional. Others were dumb, according to me—they walked with their eyes wide shut. When you see a Lucent, a Ferrari, a Lamborghini or a Shell logo hoarding, you have to be either blind or indifferent or just not bothered that you are not able to register it.

What you and I see on our journeys to work will most likely be completely different. It depends on where your mind and your observation quotient are. If you take the time to pay more attention to the stuff that is happening around you, it can open up all sorts of insights that you might not have seen before and enhance your day-to-day life positively. It takes you miles ahead of others.

Learn From Your Mom and Dad About Their Job

Get some idea about what they do at work. You can sometimes visit their office if possible. Seeing is learning.

If you don't do this, you are a dead dumb duck. How can you be so disinterested and unconcerned? And you want to do well and compete with the world? Give me a break.

If your father is a marketing head in an FMCG company, you have a walking encyclopedia at home! Can't you see that? If you request your dad to give you a broad idea of what marketing is, he will be able to fill you with loads of information—a golden learning from a hands-on master. Ask him if he could take you along and show you how things are sold. If he is a GM in a hotel, you can learn about the nuances of running a hotel. If he is a GM in railways, you should be an expert in railways, staying under the same roof! Is this not true? Is this not possible?

Go to his office and ask him to take you to each department, and you will understand how people work, make a living and run a business. Don't waste your entire time on silly gossip or WhatsApp chats. If you want to learn, this is the best way.

Our graduation gives you enough free time, in fact, more than enough time for you to invest in yourself. If your father has a business, go and learn his trade. It could be a small clinic, a factory, a warehouse or a small shop. What good is your graduation if you cannot help him make his business manifold? This will also help you crack an interview for a competitive exam or a job. This is what we look for in a young applicant.

What Movies to Watch

A film director, along with the producer, takes months and sometimes years to make a film. Every film besides entertainment has some message to convey—most do.

In addition, there are so many actors who give their lives to the cinema; then there are music directors, dialogue writers, screenplay writers, editors, costume designers, singers, choreographers, and so many who work with the logistics and production. It is an entireindustry.

By all means, watch all movies for fun, too, but always try to understand the basic thread of the movie and the purpose of it. Does it give a subtle social message? Or a moral value that is important to all? Watch all types of movies, as each delivers a message and lasting impression to remember forever. After watching a movie, you should try to write a review like an expert. You need not be a trained film critic, but you can always give your own assessment. Make a short 250–500-word review for your own sake. This will improve your articulation skills.

Some of the classic films by Indian directors are very good. At the same time, you could watch Hollywood classics too. If you have a problem understanding English, you can have subtitles. Indirectly, you will improve your English too. Today, all this is possible to watch at home on your TV and the OTT platforms.

Listen to the Radio—What to Listen

Radio is an important device if you want to improve your understanding of things and your imagination. Let me explain. During the ’60s and ’70s, there was no TV in India and cricket commentary was only available on radio. One would enjoy a match listening to the radio commentary. The excitement in the commentator’s voice would indicate and enable us to envision what was happening on the field.

If you want to improve your diction in a language, radio is again the best bet. For English, listen to BBC News and BBC World Service. Even All India Radio provides news in English. This is to improve your pronunciation, language diction and speech. Invest in a small transistor, and at a meagre cost, you can listen to the radio in your hostel room or even travel. Consider other means as well, as technology is advancing rapidly. TV usually is unavailable in hostel rooms or while travelling on a train or bus.

Go for Seminars and Workshops

If you live in a metro or a state capital, you will get an opportunity to attend free seminars conducted by various organizations on multiple subjects. These events give you the current trends and in-depth knowledge of topics like mental health, cryptocurrency, geopolitical situations, solar energy, environment, startup insights, finance, marketing, and the list is long. They get the best speakers and subject experts, and this interaction is not available anywhere. You also get to see how big events are organized. You have free meditation and yoga discussions. Photography and art are also covered. You have to keep looking out for events in your city and pick any one of your choices. In fact, go for things you don't know or are not aware of.

Interview Tip: Use these as talking points in the interview and mention them in your résumé, too.

Go for Exhibitions and Management Fares

Go to book fairs and exhibitions, housing ideas, telecom, education or agriculture. These are very engaging and a great learning experience. Good guys make short notes and make a brief write-up in a diary. Remember, you are adding value to yourself.

Many professional organizations like CII, FICCI and NASSCOM have regular meetings. These give you a rich learning experience. These are opportunities to meet people and make a good network of professionals.

There are city-wise literary festivals (Lit Fest) and book fairs. These are great learning experiences.

I can tell you that I made it a point to attend the telecom exhibition in Pragati Maidan, New Delhi, while writing a book on telecom. I got so much product information and technical inputs that were unavailable otherwise. I got a chance to meet foreign vendors and their senior teams to discuss certain aspects.

Apply for a job to know your worth learn/estimate.

Go for Interviews—It is a Learning Ground, and You Get Experience

I observe that most young girls and boys do not know their worth. They mostly have misplaced estimations about their employability. They just think of some random figure that they believe they deserve. It is good to check your own market worth by applying for a job. You will be lucky if you are called for an interview. If you are, then take an interview for an experience. Go for it seriously and see what you are offered. This is a reality check. It sounds harsh, but you have to face the reality. The earlier, the better, so that it doesn't disappoint you in real life.

When I interview graduates, they have very unrealistic expectations regarding their salary and compensation. When you ask them why they should pay you this much, they cannot justify it. There is a big gap between what you expect and what you get according to your worth. The whole idea of this book is to add to your net worth.

Some books and people mislead you by telling you that you are very good and can win anything, and you need to just be confident, and you will succeed. Let me tell you, this is the biggest sin and disservice by an author or a mentor to young graduates.

Learn About India and Great Indian Personalities

Let me assure you that India is changing fast and for good. Many people are looking within, and many Indians from abroad are returning home.

In interviews, the panel is looking for 'Indian-ness'. Are you aware of your own country? Have you read about some great Indians? Have you read about Subhash Chandra Bose, C. V. Raman, Vivekananda, Abdul Kalam, J.R.D Tata, Ambedkar,

Rabindranath Tagore, Srinivasa Ramanujan, Bankim Chandra Chattopadhyay, Ravi Shankar, Satyajit Ray, Sri Aurobindo, Satyendra Nath Bose and many such people?

> *"I have been impressed with the urgency of doing. Knowing is not enough; we must apply. Being willing is not enough; we must do".*
>
> —Leonardo da Vinci

Interview Tip

If you read about even five of them and make it your talking point in your interview, you stand head and shoulders above the rest, and this alone can become your USP and a great hobby to be reflected in your CV.

4
Pride, Motivation and Self-Esteem

"You yourself, as much as anybody in the entire universe, deserve your love and affection".

—Sharon Salzberg

These three are interlinked qualities or human traits.

If you do not have self-esteem, you will not be proud of yourself, and if you are not proud, then you will not remain motivated.

Self-esteem means respecting yourself for who you are as a complete package. No one is perfect, but God has been kind to every human being, and therefore, each one of us has several good qualities we can be proud of or feel good about. For example, someone may be slightly overweight but has a beautiful voice and sings exceptionally well. Such a person should take this skill as their USP and be happy about themselves.

Therefore, one should look at the positive side of their persona and then make a self-assessment. Do not focus on your weaknesses, or else you will get demoralized. This does not mean you do not make efforts in areas that you consider your weak points. Look at yourself holistically.

In this book, our focus is on how to get ready for a job, which also means how to make a good impression on the interviewing panel. And this is where building strong self-esteem plays a crucial role.

How can you impress people within a short time, in a brief meeting of a few minutes? Is it possible?

Yes, provided you are ready for it. In fact, when you meet someone casually or for a formal interview, the impression is formed about you within the first few minutes. Therefore, understanding what is expected from you is all the more important.

I have interviewed thousands of students as well as corporate executives. What I learnt from these interactions is that people who come for interviews are not aware of the very basics. There are three basic dimensions of one's personality. This is not only for an interview but also applicable to our social interactions as well.

- Your confidence level
- Your appearance, dressing up and so forth
- How you speak and what to communicate (ability to articulate or speak clearly and the command over the language.)

Let us take these one by one. Some of the suggestions look very simple, but most people forget them.

1. Understand the difference between 'confident' and 'overconfident' and 'esteem' versus 'arrogance': A confident person is easily spotted and commands attention within the first few minutes of the interaction. Remember, the panel members in the interview are much more mature and, in many ways, wiser than you. There's a healthy balance between too little and too much self-worth. If you cook a vegetable, you must ensure that ingredients, such as salt, pepper and masalas, are in the correct proportion. Even if one of the ingredients is not right, you will end up with a vegetable you can't eat.

So, keep the following points in mind:

- Know the difference between 'confidence' and 'arrogance'. People who are arrogant will always fail; no one likes arrogance. Be confident yet polite and respectful.
- If you are good and confident about your abilities, you shouldn't fear feedback, whether good or bad.

If you accept your weakness or shortcomings, people appreciate it.

- Do not try over-pleasing.
- You shouldn't always avoid or fear conflict or confrontation. You should be able to face people who disagree with you. Winning or losing an argument is secondary.
- You should know where to stop and where to push and be able to set boundaries and lines or limits.
- You must be able to voice your needs and opinions.
- You should have your opinions and be assertive in your argument. This reflects self-confidence. But remember to not be rude or become a pushover.
- A confident person is not afraid of setbacks and failures. Remember, if you attempt ten things, you are bound to be wrong about one or two, but appreciate the eighth or ninth you've got right.
- Such a person never feels inferior compared to others.
- Accept yourself as a package that is not perfect but has some good qualities and some not-so-good. This makes you unique; accept that.

> *"Over-confidence is the way to give your soul to the devil an inch at a time".*
>
> —Joe R. Lansdale

2. Appearance matters: Be well dressed all the time and be proud of it. Make it a habit, not just a power dressing session only for an interview. This way, you will not feel out of place during an interview. I have seen some people wearing jeans and floater sandals, uncombed hair and unshaven faces for an interview. This puts you off to interviewers and shows you are not serious about the job. A three-piece suit isn't necessary, but a neatly pressed shirt, trousers and a tie would look suitable for any occasion. A proper haircut, shave and polished shoes will give you an edge.

3. How do you communicate?: Whenever you speak, make sure you structure your thoughts in a logical flow. If you have time to prepare, write down your points. First, discuss the most important ones and handle the less important ones later. Don't speak too fast, give pauses in between, and let the other person understand your point before you move to the next one. Whatever you are discussing must be clear in your mind, and you should be able to say it with confidence and absolute clarity. It is essential to look into the eyes of people when you speak. This makes a lasting impact and shows your confidence. It is important to look cheerful and not glum-faced. On appropriate occasions, you can smile, too—it helps.

Even if you have to make a formal presentation, avoid using PowerPoint unless it's mandatory. I have seen people making fifty slides for a fifteen-minute meeting, putting the audience to sleep. Connect with the people emotionally by modulating your voice and using appropriate body language or your hands to express yourself. Rehearse in front of a mirror. Remember, the best speakers of the world, like Winston Churchill, Swami Vivekananda and PM Narendra Modi, never used PowerPoint; they are the most revered till date.

What you speak is very important!

This is where the grasp of the subject is vital. In everyday life, we don't speak about physics or chemistry. We usually talk about topics of social interest. That is why it is crucial to be worldly-wise. The best place to get general knowledge is to read newspapers, magazines and books regularly. Articulation and how you speak may require a little care and effort to develop, but developing a sound knowledge base takes *a long time and has to build up from your schooldays*. In case you want to score a point over others and make a lasting impression, I would say this has 80 per cent weightage and the first two only 20 per cent.

The best trick is to work on all the three points at the same time. The more you speak, meet people and participate in discussions with friends, the more confident you will become. Please remember that you cannot learn to swim by watching a gold medalist swimming in the pool. You've got to get inside the pool.

Before I finish, I would like to say that it is very helpful to listen to great speakers. Listen to interviews of successful people to see how they say and what they say. The best way is to learn from others.

> *"It's better to be thought a fool than to open your mouth and remove all doubt".*
>
> —Mark Twain

4. Have some aim in life. Keep it open: Some people are late in realizing their dreams or goals; many make decisions in school. I recommend something in between, which means that you may have an ambition right from childhood, but keep it a little open-ended. When you are a teenager in a school or even in a college, you are not mature enough to understand all your strengths and weaknesses, your likes and dislikes, or even your potential to do certain things. Life and ambitions are not a hundred-meter sprint but a marathon. So run along and gradually discover your likes and dislikes. Also, remember that today, opportunities are changing all the time. What you see in the next five years may not be in existence today. So, keep your eyes and ears open all the time—which door may open, you never know.

> *"The secret of success in life is for a man to be ready for his opportunity when it comes".*
>
> —Benjamin Disraeli

5. Always remain alert and inquisitive: Let me tell you there is nothing more important for success than your hunger to learn and observe. You must be inquisitive like a five-year-old child.

Read what is available on the internet and watch news channels to see where the industry, the economy, opportunities and the direction of the government are moving!

6. Keep checking your performance: Before your employer does an appraisal after one year, it is better to keep checking your performance on your own. There are several innovative ways to do it. The short story below gives you an idea of how to go about it.

A little boy went to a telephone booth, which was at the cash counter of a store, and he dialed a number. The store owner observed and listened to the conversation:

Boy: Madam, can you give me the job of cutting your lawn?

Woman (at the other end of the phone line): I already have someone to mow my lawn.

Boy: Madam, I will mow your lawn for half the price of the person who mows your lawn now.

Woman: I'm very satisfied with the person who is presently mowing the lawn.

Boy (with more perseverance): Madam, I'll even sweep the floor and the stairs of your house for free.

Woman: No, thank you!

With a smile, the little boy put the receiver down. The store owner, who was listening to all this, walked over to the boy.

Store owner: Son, I like your attitude; I like that positive spirit and would like to offer you a job.

Boy: No, thanks!

Store owner: But you were pleading for one.

Boy: No, sir, I was just checking my performance at the job I already have. I am the one who is working for that lady I was talking to!

> *"I think pride is more important sometimes than making money".*
>
> —Kapil Dev

This is called 'self-appraisal'.

5
Get Organized

"For every minute spent organizing, an hour is earned".

—Benjamin Franklin

Do you forget to take your charger from home when you go to the office? Do you often forget to put your laptop and your phone on charging at night? If you do, then it shows you are disorganized.

Some people tend to be simply careless. They would not switch off the fan or lights when they leave their bedroom. Such people have their room and cupboard always in a mess. They leave dirty plates, glasses and empty bottles on the dining table. Their toilet is always a mess. Their study table is never organized.

How do you look at such people, and what would you call them? They are not just careless; they couldn't care less. Would you like to work under a disorganized boss who keeps looking for his folders and files, who forgets to carry a notebook or pen and his notes and says, 'Oh hell, I forgot the pen drive with the presentation; run and get it from my office just as you enter the boardroom'? Such people are a pain as well as an embarrassment. Would you have a team member in your team who is like this? No way!

Then this rule applies to you, too. No one wants a careless, disorganized, forgetful fellow. This leads to being irresponsible as well. You cannot tell your boss just before the important presentation that you forgot to bring your laptop—you will get fired.

The Organized Angels

Yes, you heard it right. An organized person, boss, subordinate or peer is a blessing.

Some people are highly organized. I know of someone who has his refrigerator very organized. There is no filth, and it is sparkling clean inside. All the jars, utensils and bottles are kept in the right places. It is full but not stuffed—there is a big difference. Whatever is to be marked is appropriately labelled. So is his entire kitchen. His toilet is sparkling clean, every piece of the toiletries is neatly stacked properly, and towels are folded and kept. You will never find a toothpaste or shaving cream tube skewed and left open—never!

Habits Die Hard and Are Hard to Get Too

All good and bad habits are acquired. Some may say, 'He is born dirty and disorganized'. This can be true in most cases. But can they be improved? The answer is, again, yes. But they have to make a serious effort to reach the mark. If you are dirty and disorganized, you better do something about yourself and work on your habits.

You can learn to be organized. From planning things and jotting things down to dumping or disposing of unnecessary clutter and organizing things that matter, you will become organized as long as you're willing to learn and practice.

Organizing your life is a skill that is developed over time through practice. Focus on one thing at a time and take baby steps as you learn how to organize your life to avoid being overwhelmed and giving up too soon.

> *"The only difference between a mob and a trained army is organization".*
>
> —Calvin Coolidge

Let me tell you, it is no rocket science; it is easy as long as you want to make an effort. Let us look at a few things.

1. Make your schedules and plan your day in advance. Write down things in a small notebook or use your mobile calendar for this. Set alarms for events.

2. When you leave your home or office, ensure you have taken everything with you. Be alert, and don't get lost. Once you become a careful person, you will be much happier, less frustrated or hassled, and will be more efficient and effective.

3. Never procrastinate. The longer you wait to do something, the more difficult it will be to finish it on time. If you want your life to be less stressful and demanding—organize as much as possible. Putting in the effort to get things done as soon as possible will lift the weight off you from doing it later.

4. A place for everything. You must have a designated spot or a holder for the TV and AC remote. You must have a holder for your writing stuff and a pad on your table. Keep things where they belong. I have seen couples fighting in the morning when they can't find the car keys. Organize your files in a cabinet in your office. Organize your clothes in the wardrobe. Remaining organized is a constant effort and not a one-time job.

> *"Bottom line is, if you do not use it or need it, it's clutter, and it needs to go".*
>
> —Charisse Ward

5. Discard regularly. Today, despite being a paperless society, you receive envelopes daily. Keep what is required and throw out the rest. The same goes for all the items at your home—clothes, waste paper, used bottles and so forth. Have you ever felt like you don't have the space to keep all the stuff you own? Instead of renting a storage unit or buying a larger home, get rid of some things.

6. Don't micromanage, delegate and distribute work. This is not at all difficult. You need to load every member of your team. Give them work, let them do their work, and then you get time to do your own work. As a director of a management institute, my job was to plan, think and strategize. I trained the entire staff, reorganized the office management and distributed the workload. Once done with these duties, I realized that I was free to do my work and that there was no firefighting. My job and prime focus were to think ahead.

> *"A disorganized workspace means disorganized work habits. A sloppy work environment equals sloppy results".*
>
> —Larry Winget

Put 'well-organized' as a strength on your CV and prepare to convince the panel that you are efficient. This can be a significant selling point.

6
Passion Quotient: Your Driving Force

"The most powerful weapon on earth is the human soul on fire".

—Field Marshal F. Foch

'If you love your job, you are on a paid holiday'. This is true for every profession that you can think of. Indira Gandhi was once asked by someone, 'How do you work for twenty hours a day without getting tired'? And she replied, 'Because I love my job'.

During his visit to the United States, PM Modi spent sixty-five hours there and attended twenty meetings during this period. While coming and going to America, he also held meetings with the officers on the plane for four hours. 'Doctors tell me I need to sleep for five hours, but I sleep for a maximum of three to four hours. Yet I get a very sound sleep,' Modi said then. It is his *passion* to see India do well, and that drives him. 'When we live for our own people, one cannot get tired. The people of India are my own. Won't I feel happy to work for them?' he told schoolchildren while taking down their questions.[1]

Therefore, passion or simply something that one loves to do, becomes a driving force for professionals such as musicians, actors, scientists, fashion designers and almost every conceivable human profession. Even in your day-to-day life, maintaining

1. Agencies, "Sleeping Habits of Seven Most Powerful People," *The Economic Times*, February 11, 2017, https://economictimes.indiatimes.com/nation-world/sleeping-habits-of-seven-most-powerful-people/barack-obama/slideshow/57098129.cms.

your home by keeping it neat and clean, organizing show pieces, planning a picnic with friends, getting in shape or undertaking an outdoor trek all require that magic word: passion.

In schools and colleges, you would notice that students who like a particular subject spend more time studying that subject without getting tired and scoring high marks or grades. It is common to hear people say things like, 'I love maths but hate chemistry' or 'I love history but hate biology'. All this connects with your inner inspiration. Passion becomes the internal motivation for successful people.

In order to succeed in life, you must identify your passion—that deep-seated desire—and begin shaping your life around it. This one act of yours can transform your life and make you productive as well as happy for the rest of your days.

Passion is a powerful expression. It resides in your heart and the pit of your stomach, maybe in the rest of your vibrant body, but certainly not in your head! It is a strong emotion and, therefore, doesn't see reason. Can we explain why someone loves the color blue and hates yellow? Or why would someone choose to eat bananas instead of oranges? Humans' likes and dislikes—related to emotions—cannot be easily measured or even singled out. At best, you can make clusters of closely related emotions. Therefore, you cannot assign a number or a figure to it, as in the case of Intelligence Quotient (IQ). Yet, people use expressions like 'Fun Quotient', 'Happiness Quotient' or 'Spiritual Quotient'.

These are highly notional and can be only indicative in nature. You can say that your happiness quotient is high or low, but you cannot quantify it.

The key to success, therefore, is to identify what you love to do, and this is doable. You can always find things that are close to your heart and thus identify your passion. The next step is to make a conscious effort to raise your PQ (Passion Quotient) threshold. Albert Einstein had a very high IQ but also loved his work. Perhaps the fire in the belly (or that zing thing) contributed more to his success than his high IQ. He was almost possessed by his work.

> *"Success is not the result of spontaneous combustion; you must set yourself on fire".*
>
> —Reggie Leach

We benefit from passion in two ways: It drives us to be and live true to ourselves. It also helps us live in complete harmony between our head and heart.

Passion becomes the key to being 'more than ordinary'. It generates that adrenaline flowing in your blood and gets your creative juices running in your head.

Now let us see what it does to an individual:

- Passion is the source of energy: Jackie Chan is a one-man industry who writes, directs and acts in his own movies. Most of the dangerous stunts he does in his movies are his own. In fact, he lives and breathes cinema because he loves it.

  Film directors and co-stars of Shahrukh Khan often say, 'This man is a powerhouse of energy', and to this, Shahrukh Khan says, 'Because I love acting'.[2]
- Passion is an inner calling: It was the inner calling that made Gautam Buddha go in search of peace. Nobody told him to do what he did. He left his kingdom and his family to find a way out of miseries and human aversions.
- Passion attracts you: A football player is always attracted to a game of football. He is ready to play in extreme heat, rain or even when it is snowing. The smell of oil paint and the feel of a paintbrush get the blood racing in any artist's veins. John Travolta or Elvis Presley would be ready to dance as soon as some upbeat music starts playing.
- Passion is something you care about: Your passion for a cause is ignited when it touches your heart.

2. Entertainment Desk, "Ketan Mehta Recalls Shooting for Shah Rukh Khan's First Film When the Actor's Mother Was in 'Critical Situation': 'He Was Full of Energy'," *The Indian Express*, July 5, 2023, https://indianexpress.com/article/entertainment/bollywood/ketan-mehta-recalls-shooting-shah-rukh-khan-first-film-.

Mother Teresa worked passionately for the poor because she 'felt' for the poor and the sick. In such cases, a person works selflessly and looks for no financial rewards.

- Passion can make you walk that extra mile: We can perform certain activities without even feeling the effort. This is one method of identifying your passion because if an activity is effortless for you, then it is a strong indicator that it could be your passion.

> *"Jupiter, not wanting man's life to be wholly gloomy and grim, has bestowed far more passion than reason. Moreover, he confined reason to a cramped corner of the head and left all the rest of the body to the Passions".*
>
> —Desiderius Erasmus

- Passion is ecstasy and love: When you see great musicians, golfers, singers or even actors perform, you see them in a state of ecstasy. The great ones look as if they have been possessed by something. You cannot reach such heights of excellence unless you love your performance.

  Amitabh Bachchan was asked by Karan Johar in one of his chat shows about the secret of his great acting prowess and his intense performances. To this, he responded, 'When I go in front of the camera, I don't know something happens to me, and I just perform automatically.' This is a state of flow, total joy and ecstasy.

  I feel passion has been given to us by nature so that we can be 'on track'. It acts like an inner compass. Therefore, it is important to understand its role in our lives and our well-being.

  If passion can change your life and get you success and happiness, then it is worth trying to find out what your passion is.

Let us see what you have understood till now.

Try to answer the following:

1. Name five of your friends who are passionate about something. Also, name what they are passionate about.

2. Now speak to them and ask if your assessment of them is correct.
3. Name two people in each of the following areas you think are passionate (your personal choice).

- Actors
- Scientists
- Teachers
- Political leaders
- Sportsmen

7
Emotional Intelligence: Secret Sauce for Success

"Not everything that can be counted counts and not everything that counts can be counted".

—Albert Einstein

In this chapter, we will comprehend the significance of studying Emotional Intelligence and developing Emotional Quotient. After finishing this chapter, you will realize that it is crucial to be emotionally intelligent if you want to succeed in life. Domain expertise and academics alone cannot make you successful until and unless you have qualities like interpersonal skills, the ability to take failure, a cooperative spirit, an understanding of others' emotions and hard work, to name a few.

It is easier to imbibe this when we are still young.

Reality Check

What are three reasons for the success of cricketer M.S. Dhoni?

What qualities do the toppers of the IAS/civil services examination have? Is it only academic excellence or something more? Write three qualities.

What are the three most important qualities of a team leader?

Why do some toppers fail in life or profession?

What do you conclude with these answers?

Everybody Wants to Be Successful in Life

To be prosperous is a natural and essential requirement of every human being. Therefore, we all want to be successful in life. A prosperous life means that one must be successful as a professional and an individual. Success, besides money and materialistic achievements, also means self-esteem, satisfaction and general well-being. Fortunately, the opportunities available to you are much more today than what was available to young people about three decades ago.

- For example, apart from becoming an engineer, a doctor or a bureaucrat, one can opt for mass communication, business management, fashion designing or telecom management. It is also foremost to understand that today, most professions accept interdisciplinary qualifications. A doctor can become an actor, an engineer can become a hotelier, a chartered accountant can become a film director and so on. Therefore, your basic qualification should not deter your dreams and the scope of your professional life. Graduation should be viewed as a foundation on which you build your life. It is the starting point, and the sky is the limit today. I consider graduation or even a postgraduate degree like M.A., MBA or M.Sc. as a good pizza base. You can put or sprinkle any toppings later on the pizza base and sell it as pepperoni, mushroom, sausage, onion, black olives, green pepper and fresh garlic.
- You may not know that many IIT graduates do their MBA from an IIM and then sell FMCG products like soaps and toothpaste with Hindustan Unilever Limited (HUL).

Therefore, in due course of time, some of you will become IT professionals, singers, actors, models, painters, doctors, commercial pilots, entrepreneurs or consultants. This is possible because today, things are changing at a breakneck pace, and more and more avenues are opening up.

To succeed in any of these areas, you have to be good at that field. These areas are going to be the domains where you will be working. Therefore, it is essential to have good domain knowledge or domain expertise. For that, you should have a sound foundational knowledge and company training.

Now, you have some idea about what goes into a profession, so let us use these ideas with the following exercise.

- List ten professions according to you that are most lucrative. Also, write fifty words about the profession you would like to choose and explain why.
- Do you think domain knowledge or expertise alone is enough to be successful in the chosen field?

What Additional Qualities Are Required for Success?

What is the secret of Amitabh Bachchan's unparalleled success? Is it only his talent that has taken him to the number one position as an actor? Or is there anything else that he possesses that sets him apart from other film stars?

The answer would be yes. In addition to being a great actor, other factors contributing to his success include his strong will to overcome obstacles, his ability to work hard consistently at any age, his ability to handle illness and perform even when ill and his excellent relations with film directors. Success hasn't gone to his head, and he is punctual, prompt and polite to everyone.

Above all, his humble approach to dealing with people has made him likeable.

> "*Life grants nothing to us mortals without hard work*".
> —Florence

Similarly, Rahul Dravid is a great cricketer because besides being a gifted cricketer, he is extremely hard-working, meticulous and can play under tremendous pressure. Therefore, acquiring domain knowledge alone will not be enough for success. You need to develop these otherworldly skills. It has been well proven that great people like J.R.D. Tata, Narayan Murthy or Mohandas Pai were successful not so much because of their professional knowledge but because of their qualities such as strong willpower, love for their job, ability to handle failure, being responsible, transparency to name a few. These people also firmly believed in values like honesty, integrity and caring for others and society.

An Overview of Human Skills

Let us look at how, over a period of time, we, as a society and as individuals, developed our skills. During the beginning of the last century, society's progress depended on inventions and discoveries like cars, steel mills, electricity or penicillin, for example. All these were related to science; therefore, the study of science became significant for our progress. Because of this, a lot of importance was given to science and technology. That is how the concept of IQ (Intelligence Quotient) to test human ability came into being. It was designed to assess the logical reasoning part of human abilities.

Gradually, we have moved towards a service-based economy, and employability options have increased. The service economy in developing countries is mostly concentrated in financial services, hospitality, retail, health, human services, information technology and education. The skill sets required by the service economy differ from the industrial economy. Handling customers, human interaction and interpersonal skills have become more important than ever before. This brings the realization that besides science and technology, other more important skills are required to work effectively. These are defined as 'emotional intelligence'.

How We Behave With Others is Important for Us

People who can make friends easily, care for others and are nice to their friends are liked by everyone. You always admire those who share their things with you. You always prefer to make friends who are helpful, courteous and large-hearted.

These qualities that are not related to our academic performance but are admired by everyone. For instance, if you are very good at math and physics but do not help anyone in these subjects, you will be very unpopular in the class. You may be a great cricket player, but no one would like to play with you if you are rude to other players.

You make friends with those who are friendly. Who likes to be a friend to someone who loses his temper all the time? In fact, no one likes people who are selfish and unfriendly either.

These are the qualities which make you popular and acceptable to your peers and friends. These qualities are collectively called 'emotional intelligence'.

> *"If your emotional abilities aren't in hand, if you don't have self-awareness, if you are not able to manage your distressing emotions, if you can't have empathy and have effective relationships, then no matter how smart you are, you are not going to get very far".*
>
> —Daniel Goleman

How We Behave With Ourselves is Also Very Important

A live experiment: An experiment[1] was conducted in an American university by a researcher sixty years ago. The children were offered marshmallows (sugar candy) in a class of four-year-olds. They were told that if they wanted to eat it right then, they would get only one marshmallow, but if they were prepared to wait for fifteen to twenty minutes, they would get two.

After this, the researcher left the room, and the children were left with the marshmallows. Some kids were impatient to eat and immediately ate one marshmallow, but a few waited twenty minutes and were given two marshmallows—one additional as a reward for waiting.

Thereafter, the researcher studied the progress of these children up to their teens and later in life. It was found that the children who waited for twenty minutes generally did better in life. They did better as senior students, were more successful in their jobs and were happier than those who were impatient.

What do we learn?

- Patience is the greatest virtue.
- *Sabar ka phaal meetha hota hai* (Fruits of Patience is sweet)
- If you are prepared to work hard and wait for the results, you will succeed.

1. Angel E. Navidad and Angel E. Navidad, "Marshmallow Test Experiment and Delayed Gratification," *Simply Psychology*, August 18, 2023, https://www.simplypsychology.org/marshmallow-test.html.

Did you know this?
• Those with greater willpower have more chances to win and succeed in life. • If you care for others, they will care for you.
• A great cricketer will fail if he does not practice hard every day. • People who are humble and simple are respected by everyone. • People working without being told repeatedly are likely to do better. • Even if you are knowledgeable but do not study hard and prepare for the exam, you will not be able to score well in exams.

Emotional Intelligence Competencies in Brief

Emotional intelligence consists of twenty competencies, as Goleman described in his book,[2] who researched the subject. It is divided into four logical domains:

- **Self-awareness:** Emotional self-awareness, which is the ability to recognize one's own feelings.
- **Accurate self-assessment:** This is the ability to know your own strengths and weaknesses.
- **Self-confidence:** People with self-confidence always come out as winners. There is a difference between being confident and being overconfident.

Self-management

- **Self-control:** This is the quality that star performers possess. The ability to remain calm and composed during stressful situations is an excellent quality. Dhoni, as a cricket captain, demonstrated this.
- **Trustworthiness:** To be forthright and have integrity.
- **Conscientiousness:** Conscientious people are self-starters. They work without supervision.
- **Adaptability:** People with this ability can handle uncertainty, are open to new ideas, and are always ready to move on.

2. Daniel Goleman, *Emotional Intelligence: Why It Can Matter More than IQ*, 1995, http://ci.nii.ac.jp/ncid/BA28658620.

- **Achievement drive and getting things done:** This is the key to motivation and gives one the sense to compete with oneself, striving to continually improve one's performance.
- **Initiative:** Self-starters, these people don't require prodding to take action. Such people take pre-emptive action and are proactive.

Social awareness

- **Empathy:** This is a person's ability to be concerned about others and know and feel their needs. Such people have a high emotional connection with people.
- **Service orientation:** Understanding and satisfying one's customer is the basic requirement for customer relationships.
- **Organizational awareness:** This is the ability to read the pulse of an organization, colleagues and friends.

Relationship management

- **Developing others:** This ability is the instinct to act as a coach. Ability to guide and help others.
- **Influence:** Influencing others is the ability to manage emotions in others. It is speaking from your heart and building confidence.
- **Communication:** To be able to get your point across to the other person is a great ability.
- **Conflict management:** How to handle conflict and opposing views of people in a group.
- **Leadership with a vision:** This ability lets you inspire people to work towards a common goal.
- **Change catalyst:** This is the ability to usher in change smoothly.
- **Building bonds:** Networking is the emotional ability that helps make strong friends.
- **Teamwork and collaboration:** They work in teams and collaborate with others to succeed.

You Can Learn Emotional Intelligence

We can improve upon our EI skills. We need to first cultivate self-awareness and understand and accept our weaknesses.

Having done that, one can start making small changes in one's habits and gradually improve these skills.

Remember, it is difficult to change 100 per cent in one area, but it is easy to change 1 per cent in a hundred areas.

IQ Versus EQ

An important point to be understood is that logical reasoning and IQ are a matter of the head, whereas emotional intelligence and value-based success are from the heart.

For example, passion for acting is from the heart, not the head. Similarly, patriotism, charity and even self-esteem are from your heart, not your head. Remember that you would like to make friends with those people who are dependable, whom you can trust and who are kind-hearted. If this is what you want from others, then others would also like to see these qualities in you.

Think and Reflect on the Following Quotes

> *"Anyone can become angry—that is easy, but to be angry with the right person and to the right degree and at the right time and for the right purpose, and in the right way—that is not within everybody's power and is not easy".*
>
> —Aristotle

> *"In a very real sense we have two minds, one that thinks and one that feels".*
>
> —Daniel Goleman (*Emotional Intelligence: Why It Can Matter More Than IQ*)

> *"Emotional intelligence accounts for 80 percent of career success".*
>
> —Daniel Goleman

> *"Out of control emotions can make smart people stupid".*
>
> —Daniel Goleman

> *"Many people with IQs of 160 work for people with IQs of 100 if the former have poor intrapersonal intelligence and the latter have a high one".*
>
> —Daniel Goleman

8
Growth Mindset

"Work hard now. Don't wait. If you work hard enough, you'll be given what you deserve".

—Shaquille O'Neal

In earlier chapters, we studied and examined the concepts and importance of Passion Quotient and Emotional Quotient (Emotional Intelligence). We also understood and appreciated the significance and limitations of IQ and other gifted abilities of humans.

In this chapter, I will explain the importance of our mindset and how it can be nurtured to do better in life. I will put it across in the context of PQ, EQ and IQ and how all these can be used together as 'winning synergy' for us to do better professionally and live a more fulfilling life.

The human brain is so powerful and complex that there can be no 'one size fits all' definition.

I have read and written so much on IQ, PQ, EQ and multiple Intelligence, and I am unable to encapsulate it into a definition.

A few of the most generic and practical questions I would like to discuss are:

What is Human Intelligence?

- Human intelligence is a mental quality that consists of the ability to learn from experience, adapt to new situations, understand and handle abstract concepts, and use knowledge to manipulate one's environment.

- Today, intelligence is generally understood as the ability to understand and adapt to the environment using inherited skills and learned knowledge.

These are open-ended, flexible and can be operationalized. These are application-oriented with no fancy jargon attached.

Who Identified the Growth Mindset?

Psychologist Dr. Carol Dweck of Stanford University was the first to describe the growth mindset. In her ground-breaking research, Dweck investigated why some people fail and others succeed.[1]

She puts it as under:

"The growth mindset is based on the belief that your basic qualities are things you can cultivate through your efforts. Although people may differ in every which way in their initial talents and aptitudes, interests or temperaments, everyone can change and grow through application and experience".

She further describes it in a Harvard Business Review article, "Individuals who believe their talents can be developed (through hard work, good strategies, and input from others) have a growth mindset". She states it even more boldly in a recent article, as "students who believed their intelligence could be developed (a growth mindset) outperformed those who believed their intelligence was fixed (a fixed mindset)".

Dweck defines the opposite of a growth mindset as having a fixed one. She describes this as "believing that your qualities are carved in stone and therefore cannot change. "The fixed mindset limits achievement. It fills people's minds with interfering thoughts, makes effort disagreeable and leads to inferior learning strategies. Moreover, it makes other people into judges instead of allies".

At Organizational Level

"Growth mindset" has become a buzzword in many major companies, even working its way into their mission statements.

---

1. Dweck, Carol. *Mindset: Changing The Way You Think To Fulfil Your Potential*. Hachette UK, 2012.

Yet people have a limited, often distorted understanding of this simple idea. Here are three common misconceptions:

- Every employee feels that 'I always had a growth mindset'. People often confuse a growth mindset with being flexible, open-minded or having a positive outlook. Everyone has a mix of fixed and growth mindsets, which evolve with experience. A pure growth mindset doesn't exist, which we must acknowledge to start with.
- Just embrace the idea of a growth mindset, and good things will start happening. That is far from true.
- Mission statements are hallowed things. You can't dismiss values like Total quality management, empowerment, equality and innovation. Yet, they are of no use to employees until the organization implements these. To embody a growth mindset, you need to encourage appropriate hand-holding. Accepting certain failures.

For this to augment the efficiency and throughput of an organization, it has to be a top-down and bottom-up approach-starting from the top and targeting each employee. It has to be teamwork.

When companies embrace a growth mindset, their employees feel far more empowered and committed. They get support for collaboration.

> *"For the strength of the Pack is the Wolf, and the strength of the Wolf is the Pack".*
>
> —Rudyard Kipling

Benefits at an Individual Level

'What is in this for me'? This would be a question lurking in the mind of a person reading this book, and it is but natural.

Let us first understand that this will neither make you an Einstein, Bill Gates or Ronaldo! Let me demystify this entire idea in simple terms.

In the definition by Dr. Dweck, I have marked the three words 'your basic qualities'.

That is your base from where you start—this is what you have. It could be any quality (IQ, EQ or PQ) or even sports or music (gifted stuff) you, as of now, stand at a particular point.

Let me quantify this. Let us say for quality X, you give yourself a 10; someone may give himself 20, and some could be at 50.

Now, if you move from 10 to 12, you improve 20 per cent. And that is pretty cool.

The person with a start point of 50 with improvement of 20 per cent moves up to 60.

You can calculate for a guy starting at 20.

It is a win-win for all of you.

Now, collectively, in a team, you had 10+20+50=80 to start with.

With training, studying and making efforts, all of you have moved up 20 per cent (for the sake of argument).

Now, your collective strength is 12+24+60=96!

So you gained individually as well as collectively if and only if you had a growth mindset and assumed that you could improve.

How Does It Work?

The human brain is the most complex thing created by nature, which no one has been able to understand, at least all aspects. The advocates of this idea say that people can improve if they believe they can.

Recall what President Obama said, which became the catchphrase 'Yes we can'. We separate positive intention or even jingoism from scientific proof.

How Elastic is Our Brain?

If the organic structure of your brain is capable of changing, why wouldn't you be able to improve? Your brain can change with effort.

Brain plasticity means that our brains are able to change and adapt as a result of experience. For example, the brain can change its physical structure as a result of learning processes or move functions from one area to another in case of damage. The word plasticity doesn't refer to plastic; it refers to the brain's nature, which is shapeable, pliant or waxy.

The most rudimentary example is when a child is born and how and what he learns. If he is born in a Spanish family, he learns and excels in Spanish; if in France, he learns French quickly; and if in Chennai, he learns Tamil! This is the complexity of the human brain and its power to adapt.

Neural plasticity, also known as neuroplasticity, can be defined as the ability of the nervous system to change its activity in response to intrinsic or extrinsic stimuli by reorganizing its structure, functions or connections. A fundamental property of neurons is their ability to modify the strength and efficacy of synaptic transmission through a diverse number of activity-dependent mechanisms, typically referred to as synaptic plasticity. This is a fundamental property of nervous systems in species from insects to humans.

However, despite intense research into the mechanisms governing synaptic plasticity, it is still not clear exactly how plasticity shapes brain morphology and physiology. Thus, studying synaptic plasticity is important if we want to fully understand how the brain works.

Now that you know what your brain is capable of, don't you think it's time to let your mind become "pliant" as well?

Keep sharpening your axe and personal and organizational mindset to be aligned for maximum bang for the buck-volunteer for workshops and interventions that your organization caters to.

The Process is More Important Than the End Result

This is another crucial shift you need to make if you want to exit the headspace of the fixed mindset and enter a more productive and happier growth mindset.

The fixed mindset is typically always focused on the end result:

- Will it be good enough?
- Will someone else do it better than me?

As we said already—do not compete with others. Every human being is different; it's fruitless to compare yourself to others. Also, the end product loses value if you don't enjoy the process.

Hard work, not talent, is what distinguishes a genius. As Albert Einstein once said, "Genius is 1% inspiration, 99% perspiration".

Yes, sometimes things do happen by chance. Some people are lucky to be born with a beautiful voice, while others can't hit a note even if their life depends on it. However, hard work always pays off. A neglected talent doesn't go far, while hard work is consistently recognized and pays.

> *"Mind is a flexible mirror, adjust it, to see a better world".*
> —Amit Ray

To make the distinction between a growth mindset and a fixed mindset clearer, we have provided this table with growth mindset examples and fixed mindset examples derived from Dr. Carol Dweck's theory:

Fixed Mindset	**Growth Mindset**
Intelligence is static	Intelligence can be developed
"I desire to look smart"	"I desire to learn new stuff"
Avoids challenges	Embraces challenges
Gives up easily	Persists even when it's hard
Ignores constructive negative feedback	Sees criticism as a chance to learn
Sees the success of others as a threat	Sees the success of others as inspiration
"Failure is the limit of my abilities"	"Failure is an opportunity to grow"
Deterministic worldview	Sense of free will

Now that we are clear about a growth mindset, let's move to the next important question—how to achieve it? The first step out from the fixed mindset is believing that you can step out of it and that a growth mindset is possible to achieve.

How to?

First thing first. In self-improvement—the first word is self, no?

The Virtue of Selfishness: A New Concept of Egoism is a 1964 bestselling book by the philosopher Ayn Rand. Rand's characterization of selfishness as a virtue hits you straight in the face. She insists that having "concern with one's own interests" is a virtue.

In our case, individuals with a growth mind are first concerned about their own growth. It is like an air hostess giving instructions to passengers that in an emergency, you should first put the mask on your face before helping others.

Some Practical Tips

Mano to bhagwan, na mano to paththar

This means you need to believe in this theory.

The typical fixed mindset always uses the same proven tactics in problem-solving or learning. It's all related to the fear of failure. What if this new method doesn't work? Just because other people around you study or work using one method doesn't mean that method will necessarily work for you. It's not a competition between you and the rest of the world; it's a competition between the person you are today and the person you were yesterday. The larger the variety of tactics you're able to apply, the wider spectrum of problems you'll be able to solve!

Effort Never Goes to Waste

Why do Indian students outperform Americans? They simply want to perform better and are accustomed to working hard.

"We are simply being out-competed by children in India and China. They are not smarter than our children. They are just working harder". Education Secretary Arne Duncan said in an interview, "I have argued very clearly, and so has the President, that our school day is too short, our school week is too short, our school year is too short".[2]

2. Jha, Lalit K, and Pti. "'Indian and Chinese Students out-Competing US with Hard Work.'" *Www.Business-Standard.Com*, January 19, 2013. https://www.business-standard.com/article/economy-policy/-indian-and-chinese-students-out-competing-us-with-hard-work-110012800115_1.html.

The Education Secretary said one has to raise the bar for all students. Noting that talent matters tremendously in education, he also said that good teachers and principals make a huge difference in students' lives.

It is now very much acceptable that Indian workers work much harder than others.

Churchill froze in in the first few minutes of the first speech he attempted in the British Parliament as an MP. He vowed to work hard and became the most impactful orator quoted even today.

Habit of Learning

Cultivate a habit of learning; there are online courses, so many books, so many articles on the net and no dearth of knowledge—Use it!

Use the Dead Time

I know the head of operations of a chain of hotels in India. He advised all of his employees to enroll in some kind of course during the Covid crisis; he advised them not to waste their time. Many paid attention to him and learned new things; those who did not wasted their time. Realistic goals are specific, measurable, attainable and time-bound. The best way to get in touch with your organizational self is to sit with a pen and paper, write down your goals, analyze them, define how you will achieve them and give yourself a realistic time limit.

> *"Look at a stone cutter hammering away at his rock, perhaps a hundred times without as much as a crack showing in it. Yet at the hundred-and-first blow it will split in two, and I know it was not the last blow that did it, but all that had gone before".*
>
> —Jacob Riis

- Embrace lifelong learning
- Believe intelligence can be improved
- Put in more effort to learn
- Believe effort leads to mastery

- Believe failures are just temporary setbacks
- View feedback as a source of information
- Willingly embraces challenges
- View others' success as a source of inspiration
- View feedback as an opportunity to learn

For instance, as an author, I take the editor's criticism of my book very seriously and always in a positive light because that is how you can make your content better.

A growth mindset acts like a Force multiplier in your competence. Every organization has a Learning and Development department. Go to them and ask them to nominate you for workshops or short courses that will add value to yourself. In technical profiles, go for new languages and new concepts.

In our MBA program, we have introduced a 'before and after session'. A new concept, but that worked.

As soon as a student joins the session, there is a fifteen-minute video recording where he is asked to speak on a topic of his choice.

After the first semester, the confidence level of a student usually skyrockets, and that is what we aim for! We repeat the same exercise, and the student is shown the level of confidence and articulation he has mastered in just the first six months by looking at before and after videos. It acts as a motivator, and a student feels he can improve. In a way, he moves from a Fixed mind fixation to a Growth mind mindset. This was logged as one of our best practices.

In good institutions and colleges, there are extra credit courses you can take. There is a minimum credit course that you need to finish to get your coursework credits for your degree. Over and above, one could take classes from different departments. This is prevalent in IITs, where students volunteer for extra credit courses. This is a classic example of a Growth mindset.

Embrace Your Imperfections and Shortcomings

Everyone has strengths and weaknesses—you must understand and accept it. Einstein was not a bright student so was Darwin.

If you are trying to hide from your weaknesses, you'll never overcome them. Embrace your imperfections; they're what makes you—you!

You must remember that you can improve with effort, which is the moot point.

This doesn't mean that people with a growth mindset assume they could be the next Einstein—there are still variables in what we can all achieve. A growth mindset means people believe their intelligence and talents can be improved through effort and actions.

A growth mindset also recognizes that setbacks are a necessary part of the learning process and allows people to 'bounce back' by increasing motivational efforts.

Some Practical Examples

The world's leading companies, including Microsoft, Telenor, Cigna and Bristol-Myers Squibb, have been able to sustain the growth over time despite the fact that several large corporations have taken the initiative to pursue a growth mind strategy.

Since this book is about personal growth and personal success, let me dwell more at an individual level as far as the growth mindset is concerned.

Many great, successful actors say that they are still learning and their best is yet to come. They learn from costars, the director and even the cameraman to understand the nuances of cinematography. You need to learn your craft in several different ways.

For instance, I am an engineer by profession and training, and the obvious choice for further studies for me was a PG in engineering; I therefore did my master's in computer science from IIT.

Then, in an effort to push myself even further and step outside of my comfort zone, I enrolled in a university postgraduate course in International Relations and strategic studies. I put in a lot of effort to succeed and get good grades in a completely different field.

New Generation Feels They Know It All

Given that this book is primarily aimed at young people, let me say from experience that college students and young professionals in general believe that they already know almost everything and do not need to listen to any advice. They take a narrow approach that I refer to as having a "Set mind". It is set in mortar and cement.

This is the most dangerous attitude for your progress. Grant it that a person with more experience has more experience than you. And experience comes only with experience and not arrogance. It is one of the major reasons for failure, especially the entrepreneurs. It is good to be confident and bold, but you cannot be foolhardy. It is your business, your startup and the effort should be to use all you have to make it a success.

If you can get some senior people just to mentor you, a lot of your effort will be saved, and failures can be avoided. 'Stay hungry but don't be foolish' is a golden mantra for success as a worker or an entrepreneur.

Miracles Don't Happen, but Some Make Them Happen

If you listen to your mentors, focus on your strengths and improve on them, you can even win a boxing bout. This a true account of a Cadet at the National Defense Academy, a premier tri-service training facility for the officers of the Indian Armed Forces, located close to Pune in India. This is the finest example of a Growth mindset.

One fine day, Anil Thapar, now in the sixth and final term, while having tea with his course mates, on an impulse, decided to take to an Academy boxing tournament scheduled to start in a few months. Though each one of his rippling muscles was proof that he was indeed made for the macho sport, the last boxing bout he had was during novice boxing in the first term. Every cadet joining the Academy has to fight in it. From the first and sixth term, much water had flown in the NDA taps. There were many cadets who had excelled in this courageous, demanding sport and had been awarded with Boxing Blue (an honor of sorts). He saw himself as a late bloomer, albeit confident, like a lion from the Lion (Lima) squadron.

NDA trained foreign cadets, too, and West African Nations did have their fair share. Indian cadets had never seen such people who looked formidable—well built, thick lips and such dark, handsome guys—who were very nice and polite. It was natural for them to go for sports requiring power—Soccer and Boxing was a way to go. It is no surprise that the star Afro-American boxers of the US and footballers of South America have an African lineage, predominantly West African. Two who excelled at the NDA the most were cadets Nunu from Kilo Squadron and Dennis from Foxtrot. Meanwhile, the boxing skills and prowess of Dennis and Nunu were the talk among cadets. Anil Thapar would have to box with Dennis, being the same weight.

Anil had the strength of a lion, but he was equally aware that boxing was not just a brute force and muscle game but more of a skilled sport, so his impulsive decision to go into a boxing tournament was proper. Prem, his close friend, encouraged him.

His coursemate Kieth, though built like a mosquito or a bee, purely because of his scientifically honed skills, had his opponents yielding to his punches, jabs and hooks. He rained them on his rivals in an artistic way. Another boxer who was equally capable was Cadet DV Philip.

He naturally asked him for guidance and learning. For Philip, boxing was a form of worship—he practiced it constantly.

The first lesson Philip received in boxing was that "There is nothing that is unbeatable. Find the opponent's weak points, understand and exploit them, press on them and be sure you will win".

Lesson number two for Anil was to work on his stamina. Skipping, long-distance running, running up the hills and boat pulling were his workout routines for building endurance. It became his mantra. In the three rounds bout, staying power mattered.

The third lesson that Philip said to Anil was to "Look into opponent eyes like a hawk—a window to his mind. Read them and understand his intention before you act". Anil, therefore, would routinely practice his punches, be it jab, cross, hook or uppercut.

The final tip was, "Your boxing starts from the first stroke of the gong, not just when you are hurt. You need to have steel in your heart, iron in your fist and an unshakable belief to win".

The boxing tournament began, Dennis knocking out each of his opponents. It did not matter whether the opposition came from a boxing Blazer or a Blue.

Dennis's brutal sledgehammer punch had the force of thousands of pounds. Sure, if delivered bare fist, it could fracture the ribs of a bull. His excessive reliance on the power of his punch was his weakness as well and was to be exploited. He liked to knock down his opponents in the first round itself. Because he didn't work on his stamina, this crucial omission in his workup did not go unnoticed by sharp, agile and by now highly fit Anil Thapar.

On the other hand, Rookie Thapar barely managed to reach finals, fighting it out in every bout and making it to the boxing finals.

Now stage was set for the mother of all the boxing bouts. The stadium was filled to capacity, not an inch of room between the anxious spectators. In the red corner, wearing a long coat, stood mocking Anil, cadet Dennis. He looked composed and confident. In the blue corner stood lean and confident—Anil Thapar.

He had his head shaved off, trying to give a defiant look that was pretty threatening. One of the officers (instructors) was the referee who said, "Let's have a neat and gentlemanly fight, touch hands, back to your corners".

Gong, for the first round to begin, was rung. The noise of cadets stopped to a pin drop silence. Dennis, like a Rhino and Thapar, like a Lion, sprang on their feet. Both of them were focused and ready to go.

Dennis looked for an opening to deliver a sledgehammer knockout punch. Thapar was calm and cool and took a defensive posture. His strategy was to tire out Dennis, who proactively came towards him, trying his best to land a punch.

Thapar backed off successfully, each time to reduce the impact or get clear of his lightning vicious jab. The referee noticed it and commanded Anil to engage. Thapar now seriously went in towards Dennis, ready to hit him. But it was not easy. Dennis saw him coming towards him and unleashed a punch that landed on Thapar's face—it was not a great connection, yet it was jarring, to say the least—Anil instantly saw together stars in the galaxy. At that very moment, the bell rang to end the first round.

The attendants rushed to attend to their boxing champs.

They pulled inside the ring a small wooden stool for the boxers to sit on. Rapidly with a hand towel, they wiped the sweat and fanned the tired boxers.

The gong rang, and both the boxers moved. Anil wanted to impress his cheerleaders. Tiring Dennis out and then moving in for a kill was not his style. He also knew that to match Dennis's boxing style and power was impossible. So he very patiently did not let emotions overplay. As planned, he continued wearing out the opponent. By the end of the second round, Dennis was frustrated, with a tired expression on his face. His strength was a victim of short endurance. He moved around like a tired bull in a bullfight, and Anil was still on his feet. The gong was sounded, and the boxers withdrew to their corners.

The thought of not knocking out Anil overwhelmed Dennis as he sat on the stool. The strategy of tiring Dennis out was beginning to show results to Anil. The final round began, and immediately, there was total silence. Thapar moved like Muhammad Ali, like one of his famous quotes: "Float like a butterfly, sting like a bee". Dennis, by now, was slow and impatient. Anil knew his time was now. Balancing himself with the ease of an acrobat, he let go of a flurry of powerful punches at Dennis. Every eye among those present, like that of Arjun, the cherished shishya of Guru Dronacharya, was on the boxing two. Dennis charged on him. Anil heard the fluting sound of Dennis's gloved fist. He quickly ducked. He saw the glistening black face of Dennis and the cave of a mouth lined with huge white teeth.

Anil was taller than Dennis, and used his advantage of reach and let go of aggressive punches, giving Dennis no respite. Dennis, who was tired, his movement became uncoordinated—responses were dulled. The spectators yelled for Anil to go for the kill. Dennis was on defense and was clearly exhausted. Anil seized the moment and landed a short, stiff, forceful punch at Dennis. He threw himself back to avoid it but it was late. He buckled and went down on his knees. This was not what Dennis had expected.

"Stop"! A stern, authoritative command was given by the referee. It was loud enough to be heard by the excited, crazy spectators. Dennis labored to stand. Referee turned to face him and extended both of his arms, palms facing Dennis. Dennis, though unable to stand straight, nodded as if he wanted to hang on and fight.

The referee decided to discontinue the bout, looking at his condition. He called both the boxers to come closer. Then he turned towards the judges and, with one smart and sharp movement, lifted Anil Thapar's hand as the winner.

The spectators went wild.

Anil, as a sportsman, hugged Dennis, and in turn, Dennis sportingly patted his back. It was an end to an amazing bout. It was a technical knockout—It is when a boxer is deemed by the referee to be unable to defend himself properly.

> *"If you think you can then you can".*
>
> —Stephen Richards

The lessons learned from this story are several—All connected to the Growth Mindset

- You can improve in a skill provided you think you can and take it as a challenge
- To get it going, you have to work hard and learn from experts
- Work on your strengths and keep understanding and accepting your shortfalls, too
- Not to miss the last point—hope to win, but don't be scared of failure

Part 2: Making the Most of Student Life

9
Get Work Experience

"Men are wise in proportion, not to their experience, but to their capacity for experience".

—George Bernard Shaw

The world over, the job market is becoming more competitive. With each passing year, employers expect more from candidates. One of the main boxes that companies want prospective employees to tick is industry experience. The whole idea is to hire a person who can hit the ground running. Companies do not want to waste three months in training a person, paying him and investing in training.

People favour an experienced employee over a greenhorn. There was a weightage for job experience during our MBA selection process: Whatever it was, it was a bonus. If one had 20 per cent of students in a batch with work experience, that cluster would gain a lot of maturity. Many MBA institutes will not accept candidates unless they have a certain number of work experience, usually between three to five years. Many students, in my opinion, prefer to work for a few years before signing up for a management program.

The Need of Attaining Soft Skills and Experience

Work experience provides a real environment where you get an opportunity to speak and discuss with colleagues, seniors and juniors. Without realizing it, every day is learning, and you learn subtle aspects of human interaction. What you say impacts the impression you make on others—it could impact your job, your promotion and your next pay hike. In college, it is like laboratory learning. You mostly converse with fellow students. Your teachers tend to make you comfortable so that you can learn; there is more hand-holding.

A job is like swimming in a high sea, whereas college is a protected environment, like a swimming pool.

Courses do not directly teach soft skills essential for the real world. You get opportunities to make presentations; the environment is student-friendly.

Your learning starts from an early age itself. You learn to communicate from being in the school environment and not so much from the classes in college that professors teach.

You learn time management from juggling assignments and hobbies, not from the teachers.

These skills are the ones you can learn and develop in the real world only, in a work environment, as opposed to a classroom. Also, you grasp them in the context of a workplace.

Although you can learn a lot from taking classes, you should not underestimate what you can learn from your surroundings.

Experience enables you to get a true sense of the work—the organizational nuances, working along with people, understanding real deadlines, the pulls and pressures and above all, the seriousness of the job at hand. College projects are different. On the job, you are dealing with profit and loss and handling someone's investment and money. Therefore, you get to know what an organization looks like, its structure, the different departments and how they communicate with each other. You learn people management and dealing with people, both senior and junior. You also learn to work with peers, make a comparison, and benchmark your capabilities with others in the organization: who reports to whom, and how is the money generated or lost? It gives you a sense of seriousness.

Work experience, therefore, allows you to apply your skills. Your accomplishments can then be put on your résumé to further your career.

What All Can Be Done to Bag Substantial Experience?

> *"In determining 'the right people', the good-to-great companies placed greater weight on character attributes than on specific educational background, practical skills, specialized knowledge, or work experience".*
>
> —James C. Collins

Getting any work experience will help you stand out, especially in more competitive fields or if you think other parts of your résumé are weaker.

The Right and Timely Entry

A graduate needs his first break, and that is the biggest challenge. It is like catching a crowded bus from a bus stand. You don't want to miss the bus; you never know when the next one will come. You first need a foothold, after which you get a decent place to stand, and then, after a few stops, you get a seat and, eventually, a window seat.

Let me give you two examples. As a first-time author, getting a publisher to publish your book is very difficult. 'Have you written before?' is the first question by an editor (if you can get to the editor at all), and if that is your first book, you are shown the door. You may be a great writer, but that is how the world moves.

I experienced this with my first book, which was later reprinted over twenty times. It was translated into six regional languages and one foreign language. But the initial going was challenging and harrowing. I needed a break from my first book. All I had to showcase was my articles in newspapers; that was all I had to show to the editor.

Similarly, a short work experience but a good one for getting a job is akin to an article in the papers for clinching a deal with a good publisher—and I was pitching for Macmillan, a 150-year-old American publisher. I used my piece to convince the chief publisher that I could write well. And that worked.

Like many first-time authors, J.K. Rowling struggled to get her first book, *Harry Potter and the Philosopher's Stone*, published. The book's name was changed to *Harry Potter and the Sorcerer's Stone* in the United States. Over a dozen publishers rejected the book.

The second example is of those who want to become film actors. They call it the 'struggle period'. Most actors who do not have a godfather struggle for years to get even a first short role in a film. People like Amitabh Bachchan and Shatrughan Sinha are no different.

Most newcomers, even graduates from the National School of Drama or FTII, go from studio to studio for years and request a short three-minute role!

They look for a break and are ready to work for free.

If you are a fresher out of college, it is obvious that you lack any work experience. Can you make efforts to gain work experience without actually taking up a job? Yes, you can. A fresher out of college is like a newcomer actor—with a clean slate.

You need work experience more than money—your first break. Even on campus, for summer projects, companies don't pay stipends; most don't, and it also depends on the economic situation and the demand and supply. Therefore, your aim should be to get work, get experience and not money. The tougher the work, the tougher the boss and the tougher the environment, the better it is.

I had a student who got picked up by Volkswagen for a summer project. He was made to work almost sixteen hours a day and had a demanding boss to deal with. But within two months, he started doing a great job with full responsibility and was later sent for four months to Australia.

This also helped him in his final placement. He was much more confident after his six difficult months with a hard taskmaster and a cut-out role for learning.

Therefore, use all your might and connections—friends, parents, uncles, aunts—to get a project and be ready to work for free. But work hard to learn the job. If you can get any job, even if it is a front-office position or an appointment with a logistics company handling inventory, loading and dispatching goods, it will help you.

A Stint With an NGO or a Social Organization

> *"There is no greater joy nor greater reward than to make a fundamental difference in someone's life".*
>
> —Mary Rose McGeady

Empathy is a fundamental human trait. Caring for others is something that is on top of the stack of the human value system. In the heart of our hearts, we all want to reach out to the people less privileged; we want to help the destitute or those who are hungry and cannot get two meals a day. Some of us do it individually. We take time off to teach children from low-income families; some of us look after stray dogs and help injured animals. Sometimes, it becomes difficult to do it all by yourself. The other option is to volunteer for an organization that is into something you like. There are several in every town; some are large global organizations, and some are local. These are started by well-meaning people to address a societal problem.

For example 'Smile Foundation' works on Education, Healthcare, Livelihood, Women Empowerment and Disaster response. Another one is 'GiveIndia', an online donation platform allowing you to support a cause of choice from the NGOs evaluated for transparency and credibility. You can choose the one that works for you and lend a helping hand. These are private initiatives and are called 'NGOs'.

The term 'NGO' stands for Non-Governmental Organizations. NGO is a non-profit making, voluntary, service-oriented organization working for the benefit of society and a target group in particular.

What changes do NGOs make in the perception and understanding of students?

Any NGO gives the youth an idea about shortfalls in our society. It would sensitize a student to the sufferings of the less privileged. It will also make you feel how privileged you are and thank the almighty for giving you what others don't have. This is lifelong learning, which no college education can give. Be it caring for the elderly, caring for animals or collecting clothes from people to recycle them to those who need it most. A lot is being done in the area of climate change, too, which gives you the opportunity to contribute immensely.

NGOs perform various roles in our society, and there is hardly any area left untouched by the NGOs, be it natural resources, finance, human settlements, social development, culture, education or even energy. NGOs have played an effective role in changing the landscape of the current-day world. They have become the conscience keepers of modern democracy. Earlier, people had a vague idea about what working in an NGO entails, but now a sea change has been witnessed in the public's perception of NGOs and NGO workers.

NGOs don't pay well, as they are more towards charity and depend on funding from large organizations or contributions through crowdfunding or even individual donors. You can expect a token salary like a stipend (for example, ₹5,000 to ₹8,000 a month). But the learning can be good. A short stint with a good NGO also gives you respect. Your inclination toward CSR (Corporate Social Responsibility) can be seen on your CV; many organizations give weightage to this. This is a bonus in addition to your work experience. You meet influential people in a good NGO, which helps you to build a better personality, confidence and a strong referral network.

Start a Small Business

> "*The way to get started is to quit talking and start doing*".
>
> —Walt Disney

Richard Branson, a British entrepreneur and adventurer, now head of Virgin Group Ltd., started a small business alone. A school dropout, he entered his first successful business venture as a teenager with the magazine *Student*. Launched in 1968, *Student* Magazine was created to provide an alternative to the stale publications and school magazines of the day.

When the magazine began losing money in the late 1960s, he formed Virgin Mail Order Records to raise funds. He opened the first British discount record store in 1971. In 1973, he helped create Virgin Records, which quickly rose to become the leading label for contemporary music globally. In 1984, he became the majority backer of the airline he renamed Virgin Atlantic Airways. Despite fierce opposition, the carrier, which started with a single aircraft, was successful.

Notice the importance of experience, even of a small idea, such as starting a student-centric magazine. Richard did not take a job but ventured into business alone. His current net worth is $4.4 billion.

You can collaborate with a few people with small ventures like digital marketing, web designing and content-creating companies to combine the strengths and make something happen. I call this *Disruptive Collaboration*. Try to get a feel of business and how a small organization can work. If each small organization has four employees, you have a joint team of twelve people. You collaborate to hedge your risk, yet you can have an organization with some clout to give you a worthwhile experience.

Live Projects in Your College

With a little effort, a college can connect with a small private company or even a public sector company to do a small live project. These projects deploy a team of students under the supervision of a faculty member and take up a specific problem of the company and give a solution. I did this with BSNL and with another telecom company to get a market survey in select cities of a state. This was a rich experience for the students, and a proper, authentic report was created for a minimal cost to the company. If your college does not do it, you and your friends can contact local companies and scout for a project, and once this is done, your college can ratify it and put a supervisor, which gives the company a feeling of comfort.

This becomes a compelling input on your CV.

NCC Certification

> *Unity and Discipline*
>
> —NCC Slogan

Though the NCC 'C' certificate is good proof of your training while in NCC, it does not qualify you for any job in the private sector. But it does add weight to your CV.

It gives you an advantage over other candidates with an academic profile similar to yours, as NCC training teaches you several things that employers look for in a candidate—well-groomed, disciplined, punctual, respect for rules and being physically fit and presentable and so forth. This also reflects your being patriotic.

> *Where RAGDA is the main masala,*
> *Where up down in bend position,*
> *Is desi rollercoaster ride.*
>
> —Shruti (in her post as an NCC trainee)

Many public sector organizations prefer cadets with 'C' certification, such as Indian Airlines, Pawan Hans Limited, National Small Industries Corporation Limited and many more.

> *"Load, aim, fire—it is not a command; it is a blessing".*
>
> —Shruti (NCC cadet)

School and College Festivals Are the Breeding Ground of Initiative and Teamwork

> *"One of the best moments in college life is college fest, where students put in endless efforts to make it a success".*
>
> —Antony Alex

Participating in college functions is a great way to become confident, make more friends, improve your communication skills and demonstrate creativity. Studying hard and scoring well on exams is not everything. If you participate in constructive college activities and do generally well in exams, too, you have a great career ahead. I experience that those who do well in extracurricular activities do well in studies, too.

This can be showcased on your CV for a job as well as any interview for further studies.

Remember the cardinal principle that 'an interviewer is looking for that extra thing or zing in you', and you get hired if you have it in you.

In top American universities, much weight is given to extracurricular activities. Columbia University, Cornell University, Harvard University, the University of Pennsylvania, Princeton University and Yale University are some of the names you may be familiar with.

When it comes to engaging in extracurricular activities, it is imperative to demonstrate a true passion for the activity and not just a passing interest in it. Always think of your extracurricular activities regarding the depth of your involvement or participation and not the breadth.

Therefore, when you take up an activity, do it with all your heart and be thorough with what you do. You must establish and nurture an evident passion and expertise in whatever you choose to pursue.

To get work, you need a job, and to get a job, you need work.

10
Maintain Your Fitness

"A year from now you may wish you had started today".

—Karen Lamb

According to experts, "Fitness is an ability to execute daily functional activities with optimal performance, endurance, and strength to manage minimalist of disease, fatigue, stress and reduced sedentary behavior".[1] It is more concerned with the body's physical state than exercise and physical activity.

Staying Fit is as Important as Learning and Earning

Fitness has two components. First of all, you cannot find happiness if you constantly feel ill and lethargic. Even all the money in the world may not be able to make you happy. Second, being unfit prevents you from working and earning money.

Conversely, people can tell if you appear dull, lazy or energetic when you attend an interview. A small investment in your health can keep you content and motivated at home and at work. Therefore, it may also show on your face if you are not fit.[2]

Everyone can undertake the following actions and activities:

- Pick up some outdoor game

1. Gaurav Kapoor et al., "Physical Activity for Health and Fitness: Past, Present and Future," *Journal of Lifestyle Medicine* 12, no. 1 (January 31, 2022): 9–14, https://doi.org/10.15280/jlm.2022.12.1.9.
2. "What Does Your Face Say about Your Health?," WebMD, n.d., https://www.webmd.com/skin-problems-and-treatments/ss/slideshow-face-your-health.

> *"Look deep into nature, and then you will understand everything better".*
>
> —Albert Einstein

People can participate in social activities, test their endurance and stamina, and learn new skills through outdoor physical activity. A half-an-hour outdoor recreation helps us relieve stress by refreshing our ability to focus. The internet, mobile and television have contributed in killing the youth and therefore, you must be resolute to go out and play any game you get your hands on. For example, it could be any game like football, volleyball, cricket or badminton which can make you sweat. Outdoor movement in the sun gets you vital Vitamin D, for which no other source exists. So, spend about an hour outside each day breathing in fresh air and soaking up the sun; be it brisk walking, jogging or running.[3]

- Join a gym: Health is wealth

> *"It is health that is real wealth. And not pieces of gold and silver".*
>
> —Mahatma Gandhi

A lot of gyms have sprung up in every town and locality these days, and as a matter of fact, they are not expensive, and one can join them if willing.

If you can't afford it or can't find a gym, buy a few dumbbells and do some simple exercises at your home daily. Give it a shot and learn the fundamentals when resources are at your fingertips with just one click, like YouTube. You do not have to have a body like a wrestler or a bodybuilder, but you must be physically fit. Martial artists like Khabib Nurmagomedov, Georges St-Pierre or Jon Jones have lean physiques and are extremely fit as they use a variety of muscle groups to execute various techniques while practicing martial arts. This results

3. Emmaline Soken-Huberty, "10 Reasons Why Outdoor Games Are Important," *Open Education Online*, July 21, 2023, https://openeducationonline.com/magazine/10-reasons-why-outdoor-games-are-important/#:~:text=Outdoor%20games%20can%20boost%20creativity,to%20stay%20off%20their%20phones.

in your body developing lean muscle, which gives you a toned appearance.

- Learn yoga and pranayama—they can be your life companions

> *"Yoga is the journey of the self, through the self, to the self".*
> —Bhagavad Gita

Yoga is a practice that has been around for ages and was created to help people with their physical, mental, spiritual and emotional well-being. Although classical yoga also includes other elements, yoga, as practiced in the United States, typically emphasizes physical postures (asanas), breathing techniques (pranayama), and meditation (dhyana).[4] It can be performed in a room at home without any special equipment. If there is a garden or park nearby, that is ideal but not necessary. All you need for yoga is a basic mat, which costs very little. The advantages are substantial as you gain incredible energy and flexibility.

'Pranayama' is a Sanskrit word loosely translated to 'control of breath'. 'Prana' means breath or life force and 'ayama' means to control. So, you can think of it as a set of practices to control the 'prana' within your body through breathing techniques.

Pranayama breathing techniques came into existence around the same time as yoga and meditation—in India, around 5000 BC. They are recorded within ancient texts from around this time, such as the Yoga Sutras, and these texts mention pranayama as a foundational aspect of yoga practice.

There are always three main stages of breathing:

Purak (inhalation through nostrils)

Kumbhak (retention)

Rechak (exhalation)[5]

4. "Yoga: What You Need To Know," NCCIH, n.d., https://www.nccih.nih.gov/health/yoga-what-you-need-to-know#:~:text=It%20began%20as%20a%20spiritual,%2C%20and%20meditation%20(dyana).
5. Pallav Sengupta, "Health Impacts of Yoga and Pranayama: A State-of-the-Art Review," PubMed Central (PMC), July 1, 2012, https://www.ncbi.nlm.nih.gov/pmc/articles/PMC3415184/.

- Learn swimming—it can one day save your life; it is a great exercise

> *"Swimming is normal for me. I'm relaxed. I'm comfortable, and I know my surroundings. It's my home".*
>
> —Michael Phelps

Swimming is an excellent all-around exercise because it raises the heart rate and lessens the impact of stress on the body. It increases cardiovascular fitness, muscle strength and endurance. For this, you need to find a pool nearby where someone can teach you initially.

It can sometimes become a life-saving skill as it teaches other safety measures such as demonstration of safety equipment, like floatation devices and advice on safer places to swim.

- Read fitness blogs or magazines

> *"Most people fail, not because of lack of desire, but, because of lack of commitment".*
>
> —Vince Lombardi Jr.

Fitness blogs or magazines have long been a dependable source of knowledge, inspiration and direction for people on their path to wellness and good health. These sources provide a well-curated and trustworthy resource to help you confidently navigate the world of fitness in a world where fitness trends come and go and information overload can be overwhelming. It offers a wealth of information that can help you achieve your fitness goals provided by the experts through their professional advice, motivational success stories and valuable tips.

Following are a few wellness websites for accurate health advice:

- Exercise Prescription on Internet (ExRx)
- VeryWell Fit
- Livestrong
- Mayo Clinic

11
Making Friends and Networking

"Courage starts with showing up and letting ourselves be seen".

—Brené Brown

In this digital age, a strong network is within your reach because it is now easier than ever to communicate with people worldwide. There are various effective ways to communicate and widen the network to succeed.

Making Friends

The ability to make friends, which starts in school and college, is the first step to networking. If you are currently in high school or your first year of college, develop a habit of making friends whenever you can. Be the first to approach and take the initiative to reach out to others. A friendly and approachable person is valued by all.

A good friend is one whom you can trust. A trustworthy group of friends can significantly improve your quality of life by easing stress and reducing feelings of isolation. Therefore, it is not advisable to rely too heavily on friends made on online sites like Facebook or WhatsApp groups, but rather consult your organic friendships before making any decisions.

College festivals are excellent places to make lasting connections. To meet people who share your interests, you can also join art clubs, book clubs and meditation groups. If you want more chances to socialize, consider working for organizations like the Red Cross, Blue Cross or even some

NGOs. One should not be too picky and accept invitations when you are invited to a gathering or an event. You can repay the favour by extending and sending out your own invitations to friends or acquaintances for lunch or coffee. Even if you're just meeting someone, you can make them feel at ease by asking the right questions and paying attention. A great tip is to ask open-ended questions and encourage them to open up through phrases like "Tell me more". Remember to always be polite.

It is important to find like-minded people with shared interests for developing close friendships with matching values. As the saying goes, one can tell a lot about a person by the company they keep. Therefore, ensure that you don't associate yourself with the wrong company, as it could do more harm than good to you.

In this context, let me tell you a fascinating experience. I was conducting a workshop on motivation and emotional intelligence for senior managers of a highly regarded MNC. I had distributed a questionnaire to the participants. Among the twenty-five questions, one was to name five of your best friends. As I walked through the class, I encountered a person who was a little upset and confused. I asked him what the problem was and I was astonished by his answer. He said, "I've just realized I don't have any friends"!

Can you believe it? A senior executive at around forty had no friends! He promised to work on this weakness and make an effort to socialize with others.

Importance of Networking

Networking is a powerful tool, according to successful people like Steve Jobs, Oprah Winfrey, Porter Gale, Zig Ziglar and many more. The most successful people often succeed in their endeavors by skillfully utilizing the advantages of networking.

In this regard, social media is a fantastic tool for expanding your audience. One can connect with millions of friends and professionals through platforms like LinkedIn and Facebook. According to Lloyd Mathias, Marketing Director of India &

Southwest Asia, Motorola, LinkedIn also facilitates networking with individuals within Motorola or the industry at large.

Leaders like Ambi Parameswaran, Executive Director of Draft FCB Ulka, Ajay Chandwani, Executive Director of Percept/Hakuhodo and Ashish Bhasin, Executive Vice-President of Lowe Asia, use these networks and find them very useful.

Networking is beneficial for both your professional and personal lives. The fact is that many people struggle with it. In fact, some people express outright dread at the idea of striking up a conversation with a complete stranger at a conference or event. People who are more reserved or shy might experience a 'conversational cramp' in their throats. A good alternative is social networking is a good alternative, which has a much wider audience but no in-person meetings.

Sometimes, networking is seen as an attempt to promote oneself. You need to market yourself even when searching for your first job or a change. For example, without discussing a car's features, how can you expect to sell one to someone, especially if you have to travel to the buyer yourself? Similarly, when searching for your first job, you are scouting for an employer and your chances of landing a job increase with the number of companies you apply to. Therefore, I don't think it's inappropriate to meet people at gatherings like conferences, seminars, exhibitions or private get-togethers.

There are some people whose job it is to connect people. Following are some examples:

In addition to creating two thriving ecosystems (On Startups and Inbound) where entrepreneurs and marketers can connect and facilitate easier lives, Dharmesh Shah was able to grow a sizable company (Hubspot). He is referred to as "Boston's biggest superconnector", and at the INBOUND Summit, he recently brought 8,000 people together.

Linda Rottenberg, CEO of Endeavor Global, has connected thousands of struggling business owners with successful executives who have already traveled the same path in order to help them find "Social Capital". She is clocking 50,000+ hours of mentorship brokered per year.

> *"Networking is not about just connecting people. It's about connecting people with people, people with ideas, and people with opportunities".*
>
> —Michele Jennae

What Do You Get by Meeting People?

When you meet people, many doors suddenly open for you. The more, the better. Consider the fact that you also get to network professionally and gather fresh insights in the area of your interest. More importantly, you gain knowledge that you were unaware of, and these insights allow you to develop your thoughts further. Your career can develop as you look for new opportunities. Meeting individuals from various backgrounds helps you develop new perspectives and build confidence. Additionally, you learn the art of communicating with others, which enables you to do better in formal interviews.

Importance of Your Alumni Network

> *"Your network is your net worth".*
>
> —Porter Gale

Over the course of twenty years, I have come to understand that an academic institution's alumni are what give it power and reputation. Colleges that do not maintain relationships with their alumni end up suffering, and their students pay the price. It is to be kept in mind that your best representatives for society and the industry are your alums. For instance, many of my students at Symbiosis University are CEOs and directors of various companies. Many are entrepreneurs, and some are partners with top consulting companies around the globe. Nearly all managerial positions within the corporate hierarchy are held by them because they are all good performers. These students have left a very positive impact on the industries that came to their campus for hiring. In addition, they are corporate influencers in a very positive way.

All reputable colleges maintain a real-time database of their alumni and actively engage them in major events and academic activities.

Students must proactively support and encourage the college administration's efforts to keep in touch with alumni. As an individual, you should associate yourself with the alumni association, as it will help you stay informed about the industry and notify yourself about potential job openings.

Some schools, like The Doon School, still have the old student organizations where students aid one another in any way they can. To promote camaraderie, many other schools in India also establish student associations.

> *"Networking is a lot like nutrition and fitness: we know what to do; the hard part is making it a top priority".*
>
> —Herminia Ibarra

In conclusion, networking and expanding your network and circle of friends is a low-cost marketing trick that can lead to opportunities in a number of ways. Be it friends, alum associations, etc., all are a fantastic way to support each other and institutions in the long run.

12

Importance of Liberal Arts

"The role of a liberal arts college within a university is to be a genuine part of that university, giving and responding to the other parts".

—Edward Levi

I am a telecom engineer with an M.Tech in Computer Science from an IIT. Logically, any further academic pursuit for me should have been in the technology field itself. But I decided to do an M.A. in International Relations and Strategic Studies. I was quite interested in the subjects covered in this two-year postgraduate course. It covered contemporary history, military geography, national security, national interest, geopolitics and international relations, to name a few. For me, this course offered a refreshing change of pace. I must say that the learning experience broadened my horizons in ways that I could never have imagined. I started reading the newspaper and began looking at the news, the society and the world from an entirely different perspective.

Let me admit that it was the most enjoyable period of learning. As a science student from my school days onward, it felt liberating. It was as if I was eating vanilla-flavoured ice cream all this time, but now I was suddenly offered a delightful strawberry twist.

What is Liberal Arts and How is It Relevant in Today's Scenario?

Though prevalent for a long time, educationists have recently rediscovered this discipline. Let me put it differently according to my learning and understanding as a student as well as a teacher. I have realized that most engineers or commerce graduates go for a formal MBA. They overlook the humanities track entirely. Even if they don't undergo formal management training or education, an engineer will continue to work as an engineer for the first three years. After that, they will likely need to take over a managerial role. At this point, this individual may not be aware of the 'other things' important for the world. Now, the 'other things' here refer to the worldly wisdom largely covered in liberal arts.

STEM—another fancy acronym for Science, Technology, Engineering and Math—has been the mainstay of education across the globe, especially in India. In this context, parents and students disregarded the arts because they perceived that they did not generate any employability. To a large extent, it was a correct perspective. In recent times, however, a lot has happened. The economies have moved from manufacturing to the service sector. Hundreds of opportunities have emerged, and there is a demand for engineers and managers who can understand, appreciate and solve problems focused on understanding human behaviour and their needs.

As Kevin Reilly from the University of Wisconsin expressed, "The failure to incorporate studies in the liberal arts and humanities, along with STEM education, will deprive the next generation of students the critical thinking skills and context necessary to address the challenges they will face in the future".[1]

> *"The reason that Apple is able to create products like the iPad is because we've always tried to be at the intersection of technology and the liberal arts".*
>
> —Steve Jobs

Let us briefly look at Apple's success story to understand some key points.

Apple Inc. has now reached a market valuation of more than $3 trillion.[2] It is the world's most valuable and respected brand.

1. Charles Steger, "Why Do We Need the Humanities?," The Conversation, n.d., https://theconversation.com/why-do-we-need-the-humanities-38640.
2. Noel Randewich and Tiyashi Datta, "Apple's Market Value Ends above $3 Trillion for First Time," *Reuters*, June 30, 2023, https://www.reuters.com/technology/apples-market-value-breaches-3-trillion-mark-again-2023-06-30/.

But the founder Steve Jobs himself remarked when launching the iPad in 2010, "It's in Apple's DNA that technology alone is not enough—it's technology married with liberal arts, married with the humanities, that yields us the results that make our heart sing".[3]

In my experience, even as the head of a business school, employers recognize the value of this marriage and search for its respective qualities in our management graduates, too. It is clear that to thrive in a society where one may have up to six different careers, business and STEM graduates need to cultivate curiosity, creativity, critical thinking and good communication.

For executing any project, having technical core skills or what we call 'domain expertise' is only the beginning. One needs to appreciate and integrate several other aspects often not addressed under STEM.

For instance, designing a building itself, the square footage per family, structural design and firefighting requirements are all known and quantifiable. A civil engineer would know these like the back of their hand.

However, there are sociological and environmental dimensions with hundreds of variables. Many of these cannot be quantified, and yet they need to be integrated into the solution if the project is to be successful. This is where aesthetic judgment and informed intuition must complement deductive reasoning, where 'other things' are essential and play a significant role. STEM has too much logic, and if I say 'synthetic, cut-and-dried approach', I will not be wrong.

But now we educationists know that the industry sends a consistent message about what they look for in a college-educated employee. They must possess the ability to write, speak persuasively, analyze data effectively, work in diverse groups and understand the competitive global knowledge environment.

3. Greg Dickens, "The Most Ignored Advice from Steve Jobs (and How It Can Be Your Secret Weapon)," *Medium*, June 20, 2018, https://medium.com/swlh/the-most-ignored-advice-from-steve-jobs-and-how-it-can-be-your-secret-weapon-3995c51d54fc#:~:text=%E2%80%9CIt's%20in%20Apple's%20DNA%20that,to%20making%20Apple%20so%20successful.

All these characteristics are nurtured in a purposeful liberal arts education. Employers want these capacities in their hires, and society needs them in its citizens. In today's world, we are constantly exposed to an overwhelming amount of information and misinformation. A citizen who lacks the broad mind nurtured by liberal arts is at risk of diminishing their citizenship.

Studying Pure Liberal Arts

This is a clear option for many individuals today, and several universities offer undergraduate degrees in liberal arts.

As these programs cover many unrelated topics and new concepts, the students may lack depth but gain a varied perspective. This helps them develop and apply critical thinking skills as they look past traditional disciplinary boundaries to consider other viewpoints by comparing and contrasting concepts between subject areas. A liberal arts program encourages students to study skills required to become lifelong learners in both personal and professional spaces. This is especially beneficial for students who want to enter fast-paced industries that expect employees to continuously absorb new ideas and information. As they enter their careers, they will have an advanced worldview crucial for professionals in fields such as education, business, management, human resources and even STEM. In India, it has yet to capture the imagination of parents and students, although there has been a positive trend in recent times.

According to industry veterans and research scholars, jobs will be more reasoning-oriented in times to come. Companies will hire those professionals who are able to assess the current scenario and predict future changes. Therefore, the demand for liberal arts graduates will grow in the coming years.

In India, some top private universities like Symbiosis and FLAME offer full-time undergraduate courses in liberal arts.

The topics covered are varied, and students do have a choice of subjects such as:

1. International Relations and Political Science and Public Policy
2. Sociology

3. Philosophy
4. Anthropology
5. Media Studies
6. Film Studies
7. Peace and Conflict Studies
8. Physics
9. Performing Arts and Law

The aforementioned is not an exhaustive list; many more subjects are available.

> *"Note too that a faithful study of the liberal arts humanizes character and permits it not to be cruel".*
>
> —Ovid

Adding Liberal Arts to Professional Courses

Given the present gap between employment opportunities and job seekers, it is a good idea to add relevant courses from liberal arts to the mainstream topics.

In fact, for an MBA program at Symbiosis that I was running, I added International Relations and Geopolitics. Managers in the making must know the nuances of international politics because in their careers, they will have to take investment calls and operations in several countries outside India. Students found these courses very useful and exciting to learn.

I feel that professional colleges must add topics according to the mainstream requirements.

What Can You Do as a Job Seeker?

According to my experience, graduates need to improve their writing skills. Therefore, I strongly recommend you take a short creative writing course. You will have to search for corresponding institutes in your area. Usually, colleges that cover journalism always have such short courses. These will help you not only in getting a job but also in your career progression until you retire.

You can also look for some film appreciation courses, which can be found online. Look out for short courses on politics and diplomacy as well.

> *"I do regret that when I went to college, I didn't have a liberal arts education. I got a BFA in musical theatre, so it was a very directed toward what I was doing. I wish that I had expanded my horizons a little bit".*
>
> —Heather Dubrow

All these are great for your CV and will position you higher than other candidates. Mark these certificate courses as 'Interests in Liberal Arts' to gain the employer's attention and further your career trajectory.

13

Critical Thinking for Students

"Critical thinking is thinking about your thinking while you're thinking in order to make your thinking better".

—Richard W. Paul

Do you know that critical thinking is one of the skills for students to succeed in school and the workplace in the twenty-first century? Students who use critical thinking can better distinguish between fact and opinion and ascertain the veracity of claims. They learn more when they use critical thinking than just a set of facts and figures. Instead, they learn how to conduct their independent research to find the information. Let us now look at various aspects related to critical thinking.

Why So Much Emphasis on Thinking?

We are constantly thinking. When we are awake, we continuously address minor issues that arise; occasionally, we do so even considering the solution of the issue because it is so minor and unimportant. It implies that we think casually, trivially or even superficially about insignificant matters or concerns. Additionally, this also implies that there may be some serious issues or problems that require careful consideration.

These are especially more crucial at work or with certain problems that arise in our personal lives. For instance, you may not need a lot of information about how to make bread or which type is best if you just need to pick up a loaf from the store. You take a quick glance at the shelf before picking up the phone. However, you need to take a decision about your graduation course seriously. To choose a course of study and determine whether it will qualify you for employment, you must take into account a number of complex factors. Even at work, there are complex problems that call for discussion and brainstorming. This is an example of using critical thinking to arrive at a solution.

How Does This Impact an Individual?

Things are becoming more and more complex as a result of the information explosion, the advent of computers and our ability to transfer, sort and access enormous databases. We need to separate the wheat from the chaff, which requires us to be mentally agile and to keep approaching problems from new angles.

We cannot think casually, especially when it comes to issues that come to our desks and those that are crucial and critical, because our focus is on professionals, how to crack a job, then how to retain it and not only excel at it.

We cannot approach complex problems haphazardly. We need to train our minds to develop a systematic, structured approach to problem analysis.

Therefore, critical thinking is required in every aspect of our lives, including school and college as students, at the workplace and in our personal lives.

What Does It Entail?

It is the ability to understand, analyze and absorb the evidence, facts, observations and arguments, counter-arguments to form an opinion and reach a conclusive judgement. Critical thinking is self-directed, self-disciplined, self-monitored and self-corrective thinking.

In the end, you should be able to effectively communicate your conclusion/judgement to the concerned party.

> *"Read not to contradict and confute; nor to believe and take for granted; nor to find talk and discourse; but to weigh and consider".*
>
> —Francis Bacon

Defining Critical Thinking

There are many different definitions of the topic because it is so vast and intriguing. I will only enumerate a few to drive the point home.[1]

- "Disciplined thinking that is clear, rational, open-minded and informed by evidence".
- "Includes a commitment to using reason in the formulation of our beliefs.
- Thinking about one's thinking in a manner designed to organize and clarify, raise the efficiency of, and recognize errors and biases in one's own thinking. Critical thinking is not "hard" thinking, nor directed at solving problems (other than "improving" one's own thinking). Critical thinking is inward-directed with the intent of maximizing the rationality of the thinker. One does not use critical thinking to solve problems—one uses critical thinking to improve one's process of thinking.
- Critical thinking has seven critical features: being inquisitive and curious, being open-minded to different sides, being able to think systematically, being analytical, being persistent to truth, being confident about critical thinking itself and lastly, being mature.
- Critical thinking could be defined in several different ways, yet there is a general consensus in its key components—the desire to reach for a satisfactory result, and this should be achieved by rational thinking and a result-driven manner.

Why is It an Occupation Necessity?

People are paid to make good decisions at work. You are constantly faced with issues that require a solution whether you are a banker, investment consultant, factory manager or team leader of a small group of employees. Every decision you make matters. A wrong decision can cost your company a fortune, but a wise one can rake in significant profits!

---

1. "Critical Thinking Definition & Usage Examples | Dictionary.Com." In *Dictionary.Com*, January 24, 2021. https://www.dictionary.com/browse/critical-thinking.

Now, these are based on so many factors that the decision maker has to apply his mind very logically and analyze in depth to make a reasonably sound decision. Therefore, critical thinking is all about making trustworthy choices based on accurate information. It is built on universal intellectual ability, clarity, correctness, precision, consistency, relevance, sound evidence, excellent reasoning, depth and fairness. As a result, employers place a premium on the capacity to think critically.

> *"The important thing is not to stop questioning. Curiosity has its own reason for existing".*
>
> —Albert Einstein

Critical thinking is a crucial aspect of any career, and it helps directly in the following areas.

- **Move away from fixated ideas:** We often believe things without really knowing why. If we dig a bit deeper, we discover that we consider them because we were taught to accept them or because the people around us—friends and parents—believe them. These are not gospel boundaries for beliefs on which you may base your career and personality. If you want to be able to form your own opinions, you need to be able to think critically about your beliefs and ideas.
- **It will also make you a better person without malice or biases:** These are often buried under layers of shoddy reasoning. However, prejudices and biased beliefs don't make rational sense, and critical thinking will force them out into the open, where they can be dealt with and removed. And this is an essential feature of critical thinking that every person in the world could benefit from.
- **It Improves Decision-Making:** Big life-changing decisions, such as whether to change careers or not, benefit from critical thinking. It urges you to investigate and choose objective reasoning over your immediate emotional reaction or random thoughts.
- **Critical Thinkers are More Content and Confident:** Every challenging situation can be further simplified

if one can think critically. Critical thinking invokes a sense of introspection, which hones personal growth and amplifies general satisfaction. At the end of the day, you can say to yourself, 'I applied my mind to this, and I did it seriously'. This way, you end up more satisfied with your efforts.

- **Keeps You Well-Informed:** If you demonstrate that you do due diligence and give adequate time and effort to solve problems, people respect you; they feel you are a thought leader.

  In general, such people are more informed than others; they take and absorb inputs from various avenues.
- **Helps in Self-Reflection:** Critical thinkers are more self-reflective and are ready to modify their views and attitudes in light of new facts because they avoid being impulsive. They are respected by their juniors and peers and appreciated by their bosses.

Three Different Types of Critical Thinking

- **Analysis:** Recognizing what is being said, differentiating the relevant from the irrelevant and connecting the dots.
- **Inference:** Identifying what is being communicated and what is not. Then, taking someone more inputs to come to an inference. Use analogies to Grasp the issue and then draw conclusions.
- **Evaluation:** Determining the worth, credibility and power of an argument and then understanding the importance or value of information.

Critical thinking—Is There a Systematic Process?

Yes, there is a step-by-step way of critical thinking. If you are assessing a problem as a team of analysts, these must be kept in mind. Here are six steps[2] to understand the process that gives us clarity on what critical thinking is:

---

2. "6 Important Critical Thinking Skills You Should Master," n.d. https://www.betterup.com/blog/critical-thinking-skills#:~:text=a%20better%20learner-,6%20key%20critical%20thinking%20skills,to%20the%20critical%20thinking%20process.

- **Interpretation of the problem at hand:** To explain the situation and ensure that everyone on the team are on the same wave length, it is important to first understand it.

  Therefore, one has to think and crystalize the following:

  What is going on? Who are the individuals involved? Who owns or has a significant investment in making a decision? What is the best method to describe this?

  From this point, you are ready to move on to the next step, that is, the analysis.

- **Analysis:** Consider each individual's viewpoint, beliefs and assumptions. Examine the facts and any quantitative assessment for assessing, comparing and tracking performance or production available to back up the information in this scenario.

  Once everyone on the team feels they have thoroughly explored the questions, they are ready to move on to inference.

- **Inference:** Before you draw conclusions you infer, you need to go to the basics from the analysis phase, including the facts to generate ideas.

  This is the stage to list possible solutions and talk about the practicality of each one.

  What can be included, and what needs to be dropped? Are there any negative effects that we may and should anticipate?

  Once everyone on the team feels like they have explored all the data and questions, they can move to the evaluation stage.

- **Evaluation:** This means evaluating the soundness and plausibility of the conclusions reached during the inference phase and examining any fresh information that needs to be factored to look for logical and cognitive flaws.

- **Explanation:** Here's where communication and articulation also come into play. Setting the thought process in context and outlining the steps the team takes to arrive at the solutions will help people comprehend how the process evolves.

Finally, what were the investigation's precise findings or outcomes?

- **Self-Regulation:** One needs to go through assumptions and assess any biases the team may have had. To challenge, confirm, validate or link one's reasoning or outcomes, it is crucial to evaluate the team's inferential judgments.

  How effective was our methodology, and how closely did we adhere to it?

  What are we missing before we commit ourselves to this solution?

  You would notice that the critical thinking process is very critical of itself. It looks at a problem threadbare without any biases or presumptions.

Issues That Require Critical Thought Process in Action

The risks of drawing incorrect conclusions from your analysis and solution increase with the size of the problem. People ask you, "Have you thought this through?" because of this.

As stated earlier, purchasing a loaf of bread off the shelf is not a big deal. If something goes wrong, you might not suffer a lifetime headache. But, investing in an expensive car carries more risks. It costs a fortune, and if you choose incorrectly, you will be troubled for the next few years with maintenance, mileage, insurance and hefty EMI payments. Even so, purchasing a home is riskier; it affects the entire family. Consequently, critical issues require the use of critical thinking.

Education is an important choice you make. This is something that is directly linked to your future, career and livelihood. You can enrol in an online course, save money or take out a sizable student loan. What areas of education are in demand today and might continue to be in demand in the future? Do you like the subject and have an aptitude for it? Numerous factors need to be taken into account.

A career decision must be carefully considered. We must develop an argument for each possible alternative and evaluate the financial, social and professional contexts. We must ask ourselves why this is the best decision for us. We must be able to predict the consequences of a choice for the next five and ten years.

Here are a dozen temperaments or characteristics of critical thinking. You need to remember these when you apply critical thinking. They are self-explanatory.

- Inquisitiveness
- Open-mindedness
- Self-efficacy
- Attentiveness
- Goal-oriented internalization
- Perseverance
- Organization
- Truth-seeking
- Creativity
- Skepticism
- Reflection
- Resourcefulness

Some great critical thinkers of modern times are:

Albert Einstein, Charles Darwin, Martin Luther King Jr., Edwin Hubble, Marie Curie, Sir Isaac Newton, Stephan Hawking, Shakespeare.

Applied Critical Thinking

I have already given a critical overview of the topic, so let us now try to demystify it by looking at it in a way that is even more simplified and devoid rigid definitions. For a better assimilation and understanding of the concept, let us also look at the more simplified version.

First Thing First—Critical Thinking is Not a Panacea for All Problems

The most crucial component of our proper and correct understanding of the real world in which we live is critical thinking. Questioning and seeking answers is the basis of critical thinking, which in turn is the source of knowledge formation and should be taught as a framework for all learning experiences. Yet it is not taught in schools or even colleges, and students have lots of data, facts and information in their heads but no means or even inkling to evaluate these.

Critical thinking is deliberate thinking and hence focuses and views the topic from all possible angles. This looks pretty normal and should come to us naturally, but it's a detailed process that needs to be followed through. We believe we're thinking critically, but our opinions are biased, partial or preconceived. The results, therefore, may not be accurate and up to the mark.

It is also wrong to assume that critical thinking will always lead to the correct answer or a flawless solution. You have done it well as long as it takes you to the 'least wrong answer'.

Building Up Skill—Mental Gymnastics

You can do the following exercises (warm-up) to hone your skills to help you critically analyze any problem. This is the way to sharpen your thinking axe and also hone your perception and reasoning. Simply put, a coach teaching you 'track events' will first teach you how to build strength, balance, flexibility, power and speed. Then, only you are ready to sprint.

Before a mountaineering expedition, you go for long treks, practice rock climbing, learn to gradually carry weight on your backpack, pitch a tent, etc. These are preparatory efforts.

Similarly, let me lay down a few important pre-action exercises or activities to help you deal with critical thinking. Enhancing these skills can boost your performance in the workplace and make you a more valuable employee.

- Learn to explain any problem to a six-year-old or a novice. This is the ultimate proof of you understanding the problem correctly. You must put it in the most rudimentary manner for a kid to understand. As he has no preconceived notion or any idea of the subject, you need to begin from the beginning.

> *"If you can't explain it to a six-year-old, you don't understand it yourself".*
>
> —Albert Einstein

- Look at it differently or go over it once again. If you see how detectives work on a case and solve a murder mystery, they sometimes get stuck and hit a dead end. What do they do? They go to the beginning and redraw the entire case to see if they missed something. They draw new timelines, view them differently and often get the solution based on the facts they missed.
- Put everything schematically in a diagram or something on paper. Make this a habit, and you get better clarity. I do this as a habit. I asked the guy to write and illustrate it with a diagram, and I feel you understand it much better.
- Learn to debate. Debating a topic is like brainstorming; you get views and counterviews, and then you can filter out the best ideas and reach a solution.
- Must mark misconceptions or false notions in your mind and counter them if and when they come up in any discussion so as not to repeat a mistake.

Critical Thinking at Workplace

Applying critical thinking in the workplace is an essential skill everyone should try to improve. It can set you apart as a leader, improve the quality of your work and how your bosses and subordinates view you.

What is Critical Thinking in the Workplace?

Critical thinking is not 'fault finding' or 'criticizing', nor is it finger-pointing. Cambridge Dictionary defines it as "the process of thinking carefully about a subject or idea, without allowing feelings or opinions to affect you".[3] Essentially, this means to think about something without falling prey to personal bias

3. "Education Indoctrination - Writing 150 Fall 2020 - Medium." *Medium*, December 16, 2021. https://medium.com/writing-150-fall-2020/education-indoctrination-c339ddab0755.

or doing things the way they have always been done. It is the opposite of 'thought status quo'.

So when you start this process in an organization unfamiliar with this, you can be labelled as a guy who is 'hair-splitting' or unnecessarily wastes time. But now, people have started appreciating this as a force multiplier for organizations. Companies need critical thinkers to make reliable decisions to keep up with the rapid advancements in technology and rapidly changing business environments. Top companies are, therefore, placing increasing importance on critical thinking skills. Today, success depends on a person's decision-making and problem-solving ability. Thinking critically in the workplace enhances productivity. It lets you connect ideas, evaluate discussions, find pitfalls and solve complex issues. The workplace is packed with situations that require teams and individuals to approach complex problems and solve those using innovative approaches.

Critical thinking is very important in three areas of business activity:

- **Leadership:** Leaders are paid to make decisions. In business, decisions must be correct and advantageous to the bottom line. Leaders need to think critically when making decisions that impact the industry.
- **Problem-Solving:** There isn't a company out there without issues. To address these issues, the company has managers and leaders on staff. The majority of issues are commonplace and have standard operating procedures (SOP). Some requests need to be handled differently because they are more complicated. It is essential to use critical thinking skills as a business leader or employee when dealing with bigger and more complex problems. Therefore, before making a decision, you must first identify several alternative solutions to a problem.
- **Improves the Quality of Communication:** Communication is a great art, and it can yet be applied scientifically. Critical thinking allows you to effectively present an argument or hypothesis, anticipate what questions can come up from which corners in a boardroom and be

prepared for them. You need to carry everyone together and keep the point of view of others in mind, too.

Examples of Critical Thinking at the Workplace

There are many examples of critical thinking in the workplace. Some of them we do regularly and may not identify them as critical thinking skills.

- **Risk Assessment:** Employees in construction, finance or insurance often need to complete risk assessments.
- **Data Analysis:** Industries require the analysis of data. While digital applications can collate extensive data, only humans can analyze and interpret what the data may be telling us.
- **Recruitment:** Recruiters need to look at several CVs and other information to shortlist the ideal candidate for the role. The ability to hire without considering age, gender and other factors shows the ability to think critically.

Exercises to Attempt

Here are two fundamental problems for you to examine and appreciate.

First Exercise

Meeting Rip Van Winkle: Most of us have read the story of Rip Van Winkle. He was a person who met a few revelries in a jungle and had a party with them. They were drinking some nectar that tasted like nice beer, and before he realized what was going on, he dosed off in the jungle, tucked nicely in a cottage.

He went into a deep slumber and woke up after 100 long years! He had dosed off in 1920, and now it was 2020. He had gone old, his beard grown almost four feet long, touching his old, tattered shoes.

He was now in a city, busting with traffic. He meets you on the roadside and asks you for help. Now you have to explain to him what was happening around you!

There were no mobile phones during his time, and when he saw everyone on the road having a flat soap-case-looking thing pushed onto their ears and talking, he asks,

'What are they doing'?

He is further confused as people are talking to themselves (actually using hands-free).

'Are these guys mad or what? They are talking loudly, moving their hands and there is no one around'.

You have to tell him that.

Now he sees big hoardings of LED flat screens on massive walls and a new girl appears every ten seconds on that screen. 'Hey, where are these girls coming from'?

He is flabbergasted at seeing huge 130-storied skyscrapers. And aircraft flying over them.

You now see that you already know these things and realize we carry so much experience with us, which Rip doesn't understand.

You have to tell him that these are cell phones, not soap boxes, and people use them to communicate.

'What is a cell phone'?

Now you know how difficult it is to explain.

'And the mysterious pretty girls coming out of the wall are just projections on a screen'.

'And how dogs and cats are coming out of another wall' is an advert for pet food. You have to tell him that today we feed our pet's special food!

'What is a screen'?

Now, how do you explain this?

When you think like Rip Van Winkle, you realize we carry assumptions and certain things are taken for granted.

You have to ask innocent questions, even very basic, to analyze a problem. Sometimes, we make assumptions as we grow up with these notions.

When you think like an alien tour guide, you are forced to take a deeper look at the things we do and things we value. Sometimes, they don't sound logical from the outside looking in.

Second Exercise

Difference between wheat and chaff or fact and opinion: Do you think you know the difference between fact and opinion?

It's not always easy to discern. When you visit a store, do you feel all the goods are worth buying? Do you assume that the shopkeeper has properly assessed the quality of everything?

When you ask a question to 'Google', it throws hundreds of answers at you. Are all answers right for you? How do you sift and get the best one that meets your requirements?

For this exercise, read each statement and determine whether it sounds like a fact or an opinion. This can be completed alone or with a study partner.

Here are some statements given below. Which ones, according to you, are facts and which are opinions?

- I love dogs.
- My brother is taller than you.
- Cats are better than dogs as pets.
- You should not drink and drive.
- Indians are very hard-working.
- My dad is the strongest.
- Electric cars are better than petrol cars.
- All politicians are corrupt.

Some of them are easy to judge, but other statements may be complex.

Try to debate each point and conclude whether it is an opinion or a stated fact.

Entrepreneurs: Stay hungry, but don't be foolish.

Startups are told to take pride in failure!

The question is, why must you fail, and is there a way to avoid failure? It is your hard-earned money, and you should try to ensure you don't lose it. So, think about this.

There may not be a hundred per cent guarantee that you will not fail at all, but if you can minimize the risk, it may be well worth the effort. Critical thinking-based critical analysis can save you millions here. Many fails for the simple reason because they, one fine day, decide to start something that is trending and, without applying their mind, get into it. It is better to think critically about the business you are going to start. You need to do a proper market survey, the money you require to start, some buffer to fall back on and most of all, to evaluate your own ability to do it. You feel you can do it just because your friend did it. This is an emotional decision which can be dangerous. You need to brainstorm every aspect in detail, take the help of mentors and listen to them. You have to do a proper SWOT analysis—strengths, weaknesses, opportunities and threats to arrive at a decision.

Therefore, critical thinking is the key to analyze your business model and decision.

Fake News and Critical Thinking

With the advent of social media and so many TV channels bombarding information, it is very difficult to discern right from wrong. You do not know what is true and what is false. It is like perfecting the art of making a duplicate product! You cannot distinguish whether it is an original branded item or a duplicate—it is like counterfeit currency.

Since the US presidential election of 2016, the phrase 'fake news' has become a reality. How can you distinguish 'fake' from 'real', and what does fake news mean?

Like a fake product, it is difficult to find fake or authentic news, separating the wheat from the chaff.

Fake news is dangerous because basis a belief that people can take action and riots can take place. Even worse, fake news that a big bank has failed can hit the stock market and cause millions to withdraw their money from banks and even panic selling their stocks.

How can you use critical thinking in news stories to reduce the chances of believing fake news, or at least start to understand that everything shown or printed is not true?

'Fake news' are news items that are either totally false or do not contain all the truth to mislead readers.

Turbocharge your reasoning with Critical Thinking.

Spotting Fake News

It is like spotting a green snake in the green grass! Therefore, it is not always easy to spot fake news.

Today, people have become so good that they can make you believe in anything. The second reason is that the person receiving fake news is getting it from several different platforms and thus believes the news.

One can easily point it out if it is created unprofessionally. It might, for instance, have grammatical or date errors or misspellings.

In May 2017, Facebook[4] published a guide on how to identify false news. Here are a few pointers:

- **You should Investigate the source:** Beware of stories from unknown sources and check their website for more information. Reports from reliable news sources, such as national newspapers or broadcasters, are more likely to have been checked and verified. It is also worth looking at the URL to ensure it is a genuine news organization.
- **Dig Deeper:** Look at the evidence the article bases its claims on and check whether they seem credible. If there are no sources given, it could be fake.
- **Check other reliable sources for the same/similar item:** If yes, it is likely to be correct. If not, you should at least be doubtful.
- **Facebook's advice boils down to reading news stories critically:** It means applying logic and reason to your thinking and reading to make a sensible judgement about the information.

> *"It is the mark of an educated mind to be able to entertain a thought without accepting it".*
>
> —Aristotle

For news websites, it is better to check their political leanings. Today, they are very clear about their stand; it is good to know where the author is coming from.

Fake news spreads so fast because we all like gossip. We want to tell everyone, 'I told you first'.

4. Santa Clara University. "Facebook and Our Fake News Problem," n.d. https://www.scu.edu/ethics/focus-areas/business-ethics/resources/facebook-and-our-fake-news-problem/.

Part 3: Be Great at Work

14
Today's Casual Work Culture is an Opportunity for You

> *"Believe passionately in what you do, and never knowingly compromise your standards and values. Act like a true professional, aiming for true excellence, and the money will follow".*
>
> —David Maister

The biggest dilemma in the job market today can be stated as "There are enough jobs, yet youth are not getting jobs, and when they get a job, they do not want to work hard. The focus of a young employee, unfortunately, is how much more they can get in salaries and freebies with the least amount of effort"!

New graduates have high expectations despite having no prior work experience and frequently with zero additional skills. They have extravagant notions—from where—that a job will be an air-conditioned setting with coffee and tea available all the time, as well as perhaps a facility for pick-up and drop-off from the workplace to homes. They believe that taking frequent, well-timed "stretch and sip tea" breaks, an eight-hour workday could be reduced to six hours. Many people have this as a dream, but the reality is different. Today, a boss might state, "Your time to enter is at nine in the morning, but there is no set time to leave. You go once the work is done". This is a universal truth.

Consider the alternative viewpoint. A person who employs you has to earn money to pay you a salary. How do you expect all that without your delivering some output? Unfortunately, many youngsters do not need a job to survive as their parents have plenty of money saved up, a few properties tucked up, and, lo and behold, the kid is the only child or has at most one other sibling. They feel their future is secure, so they feel free to act foolishly. This is a fact learned out of forty years of experience in dealing with both parents and the industry. Indian parents pamper their kids a lot (some may not like this remark), but I have to be honest in my assessment and experience—no?

I have seen B.Com graduates with no interpersonal skills, extracurricular interests beyond reading, and music, and no interest in work or learning but a big spark to earn! Ask them what they think their worth is, and pat comes a reply, "At least fifty thousand rupees a month"! "Why would someone give you this much money? What can you do for me to earn a hundred thousand rupees per month to pay you fifty"?, I enquire. And there is no response. Once more, they would respond, "I will work hard and learn". My usual response in this scenario is, "You are only twenty-two years old, and you didn't put in as much effort for as long. How will you exert yourself and mature into a stallion in the next two months? Besides, I am not here to teach you everything; I am hiring an asset and not a liability"!

When reality hits them, they start working for ten or fifteen thousand per month, and they still feel they are great and are being paid less.

As a result, many young people who are just entering the workforce do not want to work.

Do You Get a Pattern?

It would be sufficient to say that the employers are frustrated and dissatisfied without assigning a percentage to such a non-committed workforce. Your employers believe—and rightly so—they must work in a challenging, competitive environment, work extremely hard to save every penny, pay taxes, operate on extremely slim profit margins and also pay salaries on time to vulnerable employees.

Now, look at the situation this way. Employers who hire a hundred fresh candidates have to pay salaries to each one of them, which requires a lot of labor. What will they look for if 50 out of 100 employees are careless with their approach, never arrive on time, never finish a task before the deadline or throw tantrums as if they are doing the employer a favor? They are searching for a few capable employees who can aid them in starting their business.

They Spoil the Work Culture Too

"One bad fish can make the entire pond dirty", goes an old proverb I am sure you have heard the saying before. Have you ever wondered how to spot a bad fish? Every third fish you encounter in this situation is bad, and this presents you with an excellent opportunity to stand out from the crowd. The worst part is that these bad guys can have a devastating impact on organizational culture as a whole.

It should be kept in mind that neither your employer nor you are doing each other any favors. For both parties to have a long-lasting, mutually beneficial relationship, it must be a win-win scenario.

Here is the Opportunity

You will automatically shine if you just work hard and perform better than the sitting ducks. In actuality, the reason the employer hired you is because you are smarter than they are. There is nothing wrong with taking this perspective. You will succeed in life if you alter your perspective to deliver and perform in an ethical manner for pay.

> *"No one can point fingers at my professionalism".*
>
> —Sudha Chandran

Do you know that megastar Amitabh Bachchan is very prompt, punctual and well-groomed, even for the early morning shift? His thought process is, "I am being paid by the producer and I have been hired for a role. So where is the question of coming late"? Despite being such a popular actor, he prides himself on being punctual and describes himself as a professional. When Amitabh began his career, Rajesh Khanna was the superstar, but he frequently missed his shooting schedules, costars complained, and the producers lost money. This was one key factor for his downfall. We cannot forget that Rajesh Khanna was at the peak of his popularity at the time, and signing him for a film was a sure success formula, yet he lost.

Dwayne Johnson, one of the highest-paid Hollywood actors with an annual salary of $270 million (1,900 crore rupees), is also very professional at work. He is far humbler than a lot of people give him credit for when acting with him. Some might want to claim that his humble act is more of a public relations (PR) stunt, but the reality is that he is a rather nice guy, just like anyone else. He can get tired and cranky, but on set, he's as professional as they come and always willing to learn what he needs to complete a role.

Over the years, Keanu Reeves has become known as one of the nicest guys[1] in Hollywood. No matter how rich and popular he is, he has stayed entirely grounded. He also possesses such a great work ethic that the people he works with can't help but be impressed as they watch him on set. As for being one of the kindest people in Hollywood, one can only say that he's done his best to ensure that the people around him are comfortable no matter what it takes.

> *"I take work very seriously and telling the truth in my job and professionalism".*
>
> —Brittany Murphy

In case of a lousy workforce that is nonperforming and a liability to the company, a hardworking, sincere guy will outshine his competition, hands down.

1. Libby Torres, "15 Reasons Fans Believe Keanu Reeves Is the Greatest Person Ever," *Insider*, November 26, 2022, https://www.insider.com/keanu-reeves-greatest-person-ever-2019-8.

15
What Is Expected from You at Work?

"The safety, honor and welfare of your country come first, always and every time.

The honor, welfare and comfort of the men you command come next.

Your own ease, comfort and safety come last, always and every time".

The above is the "Chetwode motto" that serves as the guiding principle for newly commissioned officers.

Field Marshal Philip Chetwode was very concerned with the modernization and "Indianization" of the Indian army during his time as the Chief of the General Staff in India in 1928 and Commander in Chief in India in 1930.

At the Indian Military Academy, he is honoured with a main building and central hall bearing his name. His speech from the official Academy inauguration in 1932 is the source of the credo of the Academy, which is engraved on the entrance to the main hall.

Let me rephrase this in light of the topics we will be discussing in this chapter. Your job motto should be:

The interest, success and reputation of your company come first, always and every time.

The interest, welfare and well-being of your colleagues, teammates and your subordinates come next.

Your own ease, interest, welfare and remuneration,
compensation comes last always and every time.

This can also be posted at your workplace. You might become a high-performing employee if you adhere to this.

> *"Mind is the creator of everything. You should therefore guide it to create only good. If you cling to a certain thought with dynamic will power, it finally assumes a tangible outward form. When you are able to employ your will always for constructive purposes, you become the controller of your destiny".*
>
> —Paramahansa Yogananda

One should remind oneself of one thing constantly. Whether an organization is large or small, all employees are hired to contribute to the organization's performance, growth and business.

A job is defined by the dictionary as "the work that you do regularly to earn money". In this definition, let us pay attention to the two keywords "work" and "doing it regularly". Let me add that "efficiency" is also a key concept, and you get paid for it. As a result, it is important to keep in mind three things—consistency, effort and efficiency. The last is how you make money. If you remember this all the time, you will never be unsatisfied at work. At the same time, continue to ask yourself, "Am I worth more than this because I can be more productive"? Remember that the economy of a nation is measured by its gross domestic product (GDP)—the standard measure of value addition created through the production of goods and services in a country during a certain period. Are you adding to the GDP of the organization you are working for? You will get your answer. Do you ensure that every customer is treated well and is pleased with your work if you work as a salesperson in a store? Is your work flawless when operating a machine on a shop floor? Can you improve? Can you be surpassed by anyone? Do you need to be fired if someone can do it better? Cross your heart and decide whether or not this is true.

The term "business" is defined as "the production, distribution, and sale of goods and services for a profit by an organization".

Let us keep one thing in mind. Your supervisor or manager is responsible for ensuring that you fulfill your obligation to help the organization succeed, whether that obligation is fulfilled directly or indirectly. He is also accountable to his boss.

You must consider yourself in the shoes of your boss. Now imagine if people under you do not perform, misbehave, are rude to you, don't come on time for work, do a shabby/shoddy job, constantly argue and fight with team workers, and still ask for a raise in pay, then how will you feel as a boss? If someone is inconsistent, on time and efficient, you will make efforts to improve their performance, and you will expect that person to do the same. Therefore, there is no rocket science in good performance. Just do your work sincerely, and all will be fine.

> *"One machine can do the work of fifty ordinary men. No machine can do the work of one extraordinary man".*
>
> —Elbert Hubbard

Some Additional Hygiene Points To Do Better and Get Appreciated and Rewarded

It is not acceptable for an employee to perform their duties in a robotic, emotionless manner. Remember that you are a fully grown human being and dealing with others at the workplace who are also humans. A robot completes tasks exactly as requested—not a penny less or more. Therefore, be human, not a machine. You must be active and noticeable, just like a living person. A machine cannot contribute as much as you can. Robots are routinely oiled, serviced and have their nuts and bolts checked and tightened. Do you want your nuts and bolts to be checked by your supervisor? Do you need to be sent to a workshop for overhaul and wheel alignment every month? I am sure humans are self-correcting and self-healing entities; we have better intelligence than robots. We know the difference between good and evil.

Bosses expect workers to conduct themselves professionally at all times, including in their speech, demeanor, tasks and appearance. The worker must be courteous to all parties, including clients, customers and coworkers. They ought to be proud of their work and ensure it is completed well and thoroughly.

It is also crucial to be adaptable. Changes in the workplace, such as new coworkers or assignments, must be managed by the employee. Employers prefer flexible staff who are able to adjust to alterations to schedules or regular work hours. Also, you need to be accountable. In other words, you should be prepared to take ownership of any tasks that are assigned to you and ownership of any mistakes you make.

While there is so much noise about employee rights, privileges and comforts at the workplace, employees must also remember their responsibilities to the organization. It is a two-way street. I once spent close to a year working on a long systems project with L&T in Mumbai and discovered that the company genuinely cared about every employee—from a man on the shop floor to senior management. I also observed that everyone displayed a sense of responsibility and discipline. A sizable workforce of nearly 5,000 individuals worked in a synchronized manner. Each worker ensured to give it their all.

Let me share an experience that my father narrated to me. He did his engineering in England in 1930 and did his industry training project in a German manufacturing company in Germany. He remembered two things that he said were learnings of his lifetime. First, the Germans were dedicated and proud workers. Second, they were perfectionists. If a craftsman was not satisfied with his product, he would do it all over again. He would do it ten times over to make the best product! In a way, every worker was competing with himself!

Consider how effective your business would be if you hired such individuals. There is no denying that vehicles like those made by Mercedes and BMW are still the best in the world, and they take pride in it. The Mercedes-Benz tagline is "The best or nothing", and they stick to it.

After seventy years of Independence, government is now giving Make in India a strong push, and we have made progress. At every level, especially the grassroots level, we must make it a culture of the best and most efficient.

If we want to become a manufacturing hub of the world, we need to be quality-conscious, and our products have to be world-class to sell in the global market. Therefore, every worker has to deliver and give their best.

> *"The best preparation for good work tomorrow is to do good work today".*
>
> —Elbert Hubbard

In conclusion, I would say that winning hearts at work does not require a herculean effort. A bit of common sense, sensible behavior and sincerity will take you forward all the way.

16
Learn to Adapt

"Be clear about your goal but be flexible about the process of achieving it".

—Brian Tracy

We can see that employers place more value on adaptability, but not everyone is naturally good at it. We are creatures of habit, and many of us discover that change can cause a lot of emotional reactions, from mild anxiety to panic or fear. The term 'adaptability to change' describes the capacity to successfully and quickly accept change and adapt in response. It involves accepting change in all areas of your life, not just at work.

The good news is changing your mindset and adapting in a helpful way is a skill that, like any other, can be learned if you struggle with change. Additionally, since it is a set of skills that employers value highly in their workforce, the capacity to adapt well to change is crucial for your long-term career success.

Power of Adaption is Omnipresent

Every day is a new day for all of us. We do not know what that day brings for us, good, bad or ugly experience. Whatever it may be, we handle it, make adjustments, accommodate and if required, compromise to move on.

Nature is great. It has given every microorganism the ability to adapt and happily survive. It moves up to plants, insects, animals and humans.

Every organism has a unique ecosystem within which it lives. This ecosystem is its natural habitat. This is where the basic needs of the organism to survive are met, be it food, water, shelter from the weather or a place to breed its young. All organisms need to adapt to their habitat to be able to survive.

This means adapting to survive the climatic conditions of the ecosystem, predators and other species competing for the same food and space. An adaptation is a modification or change in the organism's body or behavior that helps it to survive. An animal may adapt to its habitat in different ways. It may be a physical or structural adaptation, just as the limbs of birds have been modified into wings or how the cheetah is shaped for running at a fast speed.

A single genetic mutation causes resistance to dichlorodiphenyltrichloroethane (DDT) and pyrethroids (an insecticide class used in mosquito nets), according to new research in the journal *Genome Biology*. As resistance to pyrethroids and DDT is already spreading in mosquito populations, scientists say that this knowledge could help improve malaria control strategies. The scientists used a wide range of methods to narrow down how the resistance works, finding a single mutation in the GSTe2 gene, which makes insects break down DDT so it's no longer toxic.[1]

We learn from the above brief discussion that nature has given every species, animal and man the ability to adapt to the environment and circumstances. If the body of a cheetah can adapt, a mosquito can adapt, so can humans. Therefore, adaption is a universal phenomenon and is present in every single living being.

Fact About the Human Ability to Adapt Quickly

The human body begins adapting to high-elevation environments as quickly as overnight, and these biological changes can last for months—even after the person has returned to lower elevations.

For the first time, scientists comparing the blood of mountain hikers have observed how multiple changes affect the red blood

1. "Mosquitoes Resistant to DDT Are Also Resistant to Mosquito Net Insecticide," n.d., https://www.biomedcentral.com/about/press-centre/science-press-releases/25-feb-2014.

cells' ability to retain oxygen in low-oxygen environments—and it happens within hours.[2]

This is one reason why people living in the mountains have red cheeks.

In general terms, we call 'getting used to it' is, in a way, adaption. Let us say you eat five Rotis for lunch daily and you want to reduce weight. The best way is to cut down your diet gradually from five to four and then to three and then stabilize at two rotis per meal. You will find your body adjusting to two Rotis, and you will not have to have more than two rotis to feel full. Here, your body's metabolism adapts to manage with less.

Another example is when you move from a metro to a small city on kob transfer; there is a significant change in terms of people around you, there are new roads which you are not familiar with, and there can be problems like frequent breakdowns in electrical supply. Initially, it is unsettling, but gradually, you get 'used to it'.

In the armed forces, the children of army personnel have to change schools every three years, and this is a great learning as they adjust/adapt to new schools quickly, and this becomes a life-long asset.

> *"Flexibility makes buildings to be stronger, imagine what it can do to your soul".*
>
> —Carlos Barrios

Then Why Can't You Learn to Work in a New Workplace?

Whenever you join an organization, you initially feel unaware of how things work in a new environment. But, remember, you have not been sent to the moon or outer space. You are still on Mother Earth but may be in a different building and amongst new people. If mosquitoes can adapt, animals can adapt and your body can adapt to high altitudes, you can surely learn to thrive in a new organization.

---

2. Bec Crew, "Just 2 Weeks in The Mountains Can Change Your Blood For Months : ScienceAlert," ScienceAlert, October 17, 2016, https://www.sciencealert.com/just-2-weeks-in-the-mountains-can-change-your-blood-for-months.

Let me give another example. Kids whose parents are frequently transferred to different towns, especially military personnel, have to change schools every three years but adjust quickly to new teachers and new friends.

I am trying to highlight that with a conscious effort, one can understand the nuances of a new organization and merge with the working methodology.

In these modern times, adaptability has become the important benchmark for survival in a business and dealing with the constantly changing ecosystem due to geopolitics, government policies and quickly altering business models. What this means is that, as an employee, you must be willing to adapt as well. Technology is the biggest disruptor. We had records and turntables to play music in the 1960s and '70s, then cassettes, Walkman and VCRs were soon replaced by CDs and pen drives, and more recently, cloud storage. After eighteen years, Apple is discontinuing iTunes. "If you don't keep looking into the rearview mirror, some new idea or technology will hit you from behind", was my advice to all my students doing MBA with me.

Adaptability opens your mind to new ideas, makes you question the status quo, and gives you the willingness to go against convention. Adaptable people welcome change as they make necessary plans to handle it.

Today, most business organizations emphasize the importance of adaptability amongst employees, and this trend will continue into the future. Most HR experts believe that very soon, in the next few years, the primary criteria for recruitment will be the ability of a candidate to adapt. If you want to shine in the job market by then, it is important for you to start now by sharpening your adaptability skills. Doing so ensures you remain marketable even in the ever-changing business environment. We can't deny that our happiness, satisfaction and ability to build a quality relationship largely depend on our adaptability skills.

Adaptability increases your chances of succeeding, as you will find yourself trying out different job roles while searching for a new job or even changing positions within your job profile.

Adaptable people are resilient. I am of the view that our success in life is built on our ability to adapt.

An individual's success isn't dependent on their education, skills or experience level. It is their level of resilience and flexibility to quickly adapt that matters. This is true in sports, medicine, business, etc. An IIM MBA graduate who is an electronics engineer from IIT has to be perfectly ready to go and sell soaps and shampoos and strategize the marketing plan. If this is not adaptability, then what is?

> *"The measure of intelligence is the ability to change".*
>
> —Albert Einstein

Remember that in your first job, you are a greenhorn. People give you a few chances to make mistakes, but you must learn the ropes quickly and be ready to adapt when a change is demanded. You will beat your competition hollow if you are flexible and can smell the coffee in time.

17
Focus on Efficiency

"The greatest discovery of my generation is that human beings can alter their lives by altering their attitudes of mind".

—Lee Iacocca

The efficiency of any functional entity is evaluated in terms of the resources used (input) and the outcomes produced (output). Technically, a machine's efficiency is defined and calculated as:

"The work efficiency formula is efficiency = output/input, and you can multiply the result by 100 to get work efficiency as a percentage".

In a nutshell, it refers to how hard a worker works and how much they produce or accomplish.

Let's say "Typist A" spends 8 hours on the keyboard and produces 100 error-free pages while "Typist B" spends the same amount of time producing 150 pages of the same quality. As a result, Typist B is more productive.

A different way to put it is that efficiency is "the system using the least amount of input to supply the very best amount of output". Working effectively leads to a better-produced volume from an equivalent amount of resource input. Therefore, the production that is occurring with the least amount of resource waste is what is meant by effectiveness.

Efficiency at Workplace

Effectiveness in a work environment would mean completing tasks and achieving goals with the least amount of resources possible.

Personal efficiency means handling the tasks according to a system without taking stress or having a work balance and never being overburdened with the work because of delaying it or being able to accomplish long-term goals rather than focusing on day-to-day objectives. It is the speed of an individual that helps to accomplish the goals under certain conditions, with specific quality and optimal cost.

Productivity, at an individual level, is the completion of different jobs in a way to achieve your objectives that brings a balance to your work and free time. The potential returns when you maximize how efficiently you work can be enormous. Some people are achieving twice as much as others are getting done daily. Such employees performing at high efficiency end up leaving the others far behind.

Working Efficiently—No Rocket Science

An organized and conscientious person can deliver optimum output; it's just a matter of being more efficient and attentive. You don't have to be Superman to achieve your goals. Remember that people above you have a sense of judgment and usually have realistic expectations from employees. As long as you are as good as the mid-level performers, you are suitable to be employed. If you outperform the rest, you can look for rewards and promotions.

There are a few things that you need to keep in mind to give your best without going crazy or stressed out. I feel this is extremely important. You are efficient if your engine works well every day without overheating! And this is an efficient machine or a human being. You cannot drive a car every day, zipping from 0 to 100 km in 8 seconds while keeping your foot on the gas pedal for 8 hours nonstop, driving at top speed. Your engine will get burned out and will seize in a couple of days. You can change the pistons and block off the engine to get the car back on the road, but you, as a human being, driving yourself at full speed with the hand brake on, will either kill yourself with stress or will land up in a hospital with a nervous breakdown.

There are simple ways to be efficient and effective in the workplace. In simpler terms, you work efficiently and not foolishly. Here are some common sense points to keep in mind.

Start in a Planned, Careful Way

Start your car, adjust the rearview mirror, release the hand brake, wear your seat belt and look both sides in the rearview mirror before you drive.

Don't just take off early morning. Take 15–20 minutes to carefully go through what your day ahead looks like and put down everything on paper (in fact, you can plan the day the previous night). Allocate time slots to each job. Now you can begin your day's work. Such planning looks like a waste of time, but it usually doubles the speed at which you do your work.

I, for one, draw a vertical line on a single page to divide into two halves and then make a list on a page in my diary. Even if I have fifty points, they are on a single page—all the time, visible to me without flipping pages.

Next, I conduct an ABC analysis. "A" is most important and downwards. You must keep things straightforward to avoid becoming entangled in a planning web of noodle. Ninety per cent my diary is painted red at the end of the day because I keep deleting what I keep finishing throughout the day with a red pen. The remaining ten per cent I carry forward for the next day, like debit. This works beautifully. The red color serves as a motivator for me—the redder, the happier I am! I learned this from one of my mentors and have worked ever since this way, and I've done pretty well. Try it. It is simple, but it works.

> "The discipline of writing something down is the first step toward making it happen".
>
> —Lee Iacocca

Lee Iacocca, the CEO of Chrysler Corporation during the 1980s, turned around the company from near bankruptcy. He said in his book, "If a CEO cannot make his turnaround plan for even a big corporation in one single page, then he/she needs to be fired"![1]

I completely agree with him.

Let us understand one thing. These days, there is not enough time to get all your jobs done. So, if you don't do your most

1. Iacocca, Lee A., and Sonny Kleinfield. *Talking Straight*. Bantam Books, 1989.

crucial jobs first, many days you will find they never get done at all. You will end up in big trouble.

Just Browse Through the Emails in the Morning

Emails clutter your mailbox. You need to spend five minutes on window cleaning. Cut the clutter—God knows how many silly emails fill your inbox daily—the sight of it is overwhelming. It's like driving with a frosted windshield in your car! So clean it up—wipe it clean and keep the ones that matter and are work-related.

Another point that needs to be understood is not to mark CC to all and sundry. I was dealing with an MNC almost a decade back. Out there, a VP of marketing was writing to his GM and was marking CC to all managers, accounts and admin too. In the end, no one knew who was to take action. It then started a chain reaction, and I used to call it "Mail mail *khelo... khela hobey*". Therefore, every employee must be careful not to create electronic litter for others to clean.

Once you have settled down, planned and checked your day, cleaned your window, it is time to respond to few emails.

Start responding to emails after 11:00 a.m. or so.

Don't Spend Too Much Time on Unimportant Tasks

You can save a ton of time by rushing jobs that don't matter much. As Warren Buffett said, "What's not worth doing is not worth doing well".

In a day's work, you have a 'to-do list'. Say you have twenty jobs to finish; there is an excellent way to prioritize these. I still use a diary and note down all the points on a page with a pen, then I review that list before I start the day and mark them A, B and C. The ones marked C are the least important as far as my work is concerned, and A is the most important. So I spend more time and do due diligence on A types and try to push C down the work priority and don't spend my time on these—and this works very well.

Work in Uninterrupted Blocks of Time

> *"The effectiveness of work increases according to geometric progression if there are no interruptions".*
>
> —Andre Maurois

Interruptions reduce our efficiency. Try and request people not to disturb up to a particular time, say tea break or lunchtime. It should be like a virtual "Do Not Disturb" board. Once your coworkers understand your working style, they will not bother you. You have to be firm. Don't take breaks; they can kill efficiency. You can occasionally book a meeting room at your office and post a big "Do Not Disturb" sign on the door. No one should know where you are—but be reachable on the phone.

Although everyone has a start time, most people continue working as if they were walking on a treadmill. They believe that flextime entails continuous stretching. This is a poor workplace culture, which can occasionally be a self-inflicted wound.

If you fix a time to leave, you will automatically stop time-wasting activities and work with complete dedication for your own sake and finish the job on time. But when your workday is open-ended, there's no real need to work fast. Parkinson's Law says, "Work expands to fill the time allotted for it".

This is efficiency in action at work.

Effective time management equals being optimized. You must spend your time on the important tasks, not just the urgent ones. We must recognize the distinction in order to accomplish this.

Important activity: The activity has an outcome that leads us to achieve our goals, whether professional or personal.

Urgent activity: The activity demands immediate attention and is usually associated with achieving someone else's goals. This type of activity usually receives the most of our concentration because the consequence of not dealing with it is immediate.

> *"Efficiency is doing things right; effectiveness is doing the right things".*
>
> —Peter Drucker

Time is a perishable item. The resource that we can least afford to waste is time. It is the most precious of all resources. Other resources can often be purchased or acquired, but time cannot be purchased. Once lost, time can never be recaptured. Time, as a resource, should be of particular importance for every working person.

18

ROTI—Return On Time Invested

"Doing something for the mere joy of it—for one's self or others—is quite possibly one of the best returns on an investment of time that a person can receive".

—Laurie Buchanan

Time truly is money, as they say, and this is mostly true. In this context, I can think of three reasons. First, lost time cannot be recovered—it's irretrievably lost. Second, you should make the most of each opportunity to do good in the world and for yourself. Third, the time you have left to do good deeds is limited.

Concept of ROTI

Let me give you an example. In a life span of 75 years, one has only 60 years to accomplish something significant. The first 15 years is your childhood time in school to learn some basics. If you retire at the age of 60, the productive window further shrinks to 45 years. Every year has 365 days, and each day has 24 hours. Therefore, you have 45×365×24 = 394,200 hours with you. Eight hours of sleep and 2 hours for eating, bathing, etc., leaves you with 14 hours a day at max. As per the rules, we work only 8 hours a day, which means 45×365×8 = 131,400 hours of useful time. This is a ballpark figure of 1.3 lakh hours!

Therefore, if you have limited time, you must ensure that you utilize every minute properly and efficiently. I discussed efficiency in detail in the last chapter. Now, let us see what the roadblocks that impede our progress are.

As explained in the earlier chapter what Warren Buffet said that don't waste time on things that are not important. I have seen people at senior level wasting hours on deciding a menu for lunch on a seminar day. This is not giving much return on your time invested. If you spend much less time deciding what soups you want or desserts, you will get more time to work on market strategy or deciding the budget for the seminar, which has a more tangible effect on your output. As Americans say, 'More bang for the buck'.

How to Make the Best ROTI?

Let us again take the example of a car and how we can better the performance of the engine.

There are a few easy things that we can do to improve the performance of a petrol engine, which is not as good as it should be. Actually, your engine produces more power than it can use to move the car. Internal friction and components that consume enormous amounts of power to move themselves are sources of power loss. And consider how much heat energy—which has no useful use—is lost to the atmosphere. You might be surprised to know that an automobile engine wastes between 70–80 per cent of the heat energy generated by the fuel. In addition, a significant amount of heat is released through the tailpipe, and 25 per cent is lost to the wind via the cooling system. We harness barely 25 per cent of the fuel's British thermal units. Talk about waste. It's insulting to efficiency.

There are many reasons, but let us look at the main ones. Cooling is something that kills the performance if not done correctly. The metal of the engine block, cylinder head and pistons absorbs most of the heat generated by the combustion of air and fuel.

If we apply this analogy to the workplace, we can say that when we argue with others, we generate a lot of waste heat. Humans perform much worse than an overheated engine, which only operates at 30 per cent efficiency. Your ability to think clearly is impaired by a heated argument (fortunately, that doesn't happen to a car; its software and silicon chips still function). But for an agitated human being, their chips are literally down. They stop thinking, and probably half the day goes to waste while they keep sulking.

> *"You cannot prevent birds of sorrow from flying over your head, but you can prevent them from building nests in your hair".*
>
> —A Chinese proverb

The lesson learned is not to get into an argument. I only took one positive thing away from social media, and that was how to cut off an argumentative person. I simply state, "I agree with you", and the conversation ends. Keep your head cool at all times, and you will work much more efficiently and quickly. We frequently get into pointless arguments with colleagues that never end, mostly during tea or lunch breaks when our mind is free and itching to do something. An adage, "An empty mind is the devil's workshop", comes into action. Talk of a movie, a book you read or even the weather, but stop getting into an argument. This is the biggest time waster and efficiency cracker. In addition, an argument that sometimes becomes heated shows you in a bad light in front of friends, colleagues and sometimes your bosses. Therefore, a cool-headed person is admired all the time.

The second one is lubrication. Putting in good engine oil makes it a smooth ride for your car or motorbike. Similarly, a bit of humor acts like a lubricant. Helping others out at the workplace acts like a lubricant. Its psychological bribe is harmless and works wonders. Most people are good and would be ready to return a favor whenever you need it. Remember that a colleague's positive input about you in the corridors of power is like a god rating. Let people rate you as a cool, helpful person, and you will surely fly.

To utilize your time, humor and help are very useful, so never underestimate their power. And you will get maximum bang for the buck and maximum return on time invested.

The third important thing to understand and accept is doing a personal SWOT analysis and focusing on your weaknesses. Accept them and then try to improve. We all have limitations; no one can be good at everything, and no one expects this from you. Therefore, attempt things you can do well and steer clear of the ones you are not good at. It is the job of the leader or a team supervisor to put the right person for the right job, but you must also know what you can do and what you cannot.

Never fall victim to habits like multitasking or procrastination. Work on one task at a time and do everything to keep it less stressful and less prone to mistakes. Keep things clear in your head, and you can accomplish much more than expected, much faster. Set rewards for yourself. Make it a habit to celebrate success and reward yourself whenever you complete a project or task. Doing this boosts your work performance, and you will always have something to look forward to at work.

Find patterns in your performance to see what is good and what is not so good.

Decide what you enjoy the most at work, which will help you perform better.

Take feedback from friends and colleagues and find out what others think about you. Make a note of how you respond to situations that require action, thought and insight—remember that self-assessment is the best assessment.

Giving my own example, when I write an opinion article for a national daily, I do take care of the editor's feedback. It is hard to reword your opinion, but it works very well because the editor knows what makes better sense for the readers. In some cases, I had to rewrite the whole thousand-word article or I dropped it due to lack of conviction. So be honest with yourself, and you will not go wrong.

The last tip is to remain focused on the work you are being paid for. There can be a lot of distractions in a day's work. Yet it depends on which ones you will allow to mess with your work.

If you want to avoid interruptions or distractions at work, then you need to keep away from your phone or email. Turn off the notification and keep your eye on successfully completing the tasks at hand. Today, mobiles have reached a level of sickness—a viral pandemic. Also, learn to say "no" when necessary. Be polite, but be firm. You can, and you must say no to anything or anyone who can interrupt your day.

> *"An investment is deemed an investment only through its returns."*—On Investment
>
> —Lamine Pearlheart

Parting Shot

If you want to be an efficient worker and you want your work to be appreciated, keep ROTI in mind. You are getting paid by the month; in Western countries, it is per week and your output is probably measured in hours or dollars per hour. Consultants of big companies do charge per hour; even big lawyers do it. So, your employer looks at you as his ROTI. You will not get the next assignment if you do not deliver things on time or while away time to charge more (more hours for the same job).

If your output in one hour is less than your other colleagues, you are seen as a wasteful employee! And if you do more work than others, your ROTI for your boss is better, and you get a pat on the back and a better appraisal. As a new employee or a fresher, this becomes a clincher you cannot miss out on.

19
Getting along with Colleagues

"I'm not the smartest fellow in the world, but
I can sure pick smart colleagues".

—Franklin D Roosevelt

What is the importance of colleagues in the workplace? Studies show that people love going to their workplace because of the great environment. The pandemic taught this the hard way—people wanted to go to the office, and kids wanted to return to school. The environment and a happening place are not created by brick and mortar but by human beings who occupy that space. Workplace happiness is all that matters to this workforce, and that depends on the people who work together.

A Gallup survey[1] shows that close friendships at work can boost employee satisfaction by 50 per cent. Further, people with a best friend at the workplace are seven times more likely to engage fully in their work and would not quit.

Therefore, it is important for people to feel that they are working alongside good people.

The opposite is also a fact that a few bad guys in an organization can vitiate the environment, which is so very important for not only individual happiness and productivity but also for the overall performance of an organization. It is an old saying that a "chain is as strong as the weakest link".

---

1. Riordan, Christine M. "We All Need Friends at Work." Harvard Business Review, August 7, 2014. https://hbr.org/2013/07/we-all-need-friends-at-work#:~:text=Gallup%20found%20that%20close%20work,we%20are%20in%2Dit%20together.

Segregating good from bad is not all that difficult. My experience tells me that it is not very difficult to separate the wheat from the chaff. For instance, when a fresh batch of MBA aspirants join an institute or college, it takes the faculty around three months to identify the good, not-so-good and the bad ones.

Six months after the commencement of the academic program, I began to form student committees. These groups of students have an important role to play, and each committee is headed by a committee head. Since this is a leadership role, we do due diligence before we finalize these names. The process we follow reveals a lot. We go for a "batch popularity vote".

A list is drawn from all those who have applied for the job of committee head. The entire batch is asked to rate each candidate in a closed room. If there are twenty candidates, then one has to mark the best as one and the worst as twenty. This is then fed into a computer to get the batch popularity of each individual.

Year after year, we are surprised by the fact that the student voted most popular by the batch is also voted the most suitable for the job by the panel of staff that selects these committee heads. What we learn from this simple yet essential exercise is that human perception of coworkers is not as varied as it is thought to be. A good guy is seen as good by "most" people.

Similarly, most teammates or peers perceive a good colleague at the workplace as a good colleague.

You want to compete and outperform others, but you cannot see these people as enemies or adversaries. Remember, you cannot achieve much alone; you need others too. You better get along with the majority, if not all, for your own good.

Let us now look at the characteristics of people that impact workplace relationships. Today, we typically switch jobs every three years. In a working career of three decades, one would have changed ten jobs on average and encountered several people in each organization—seeing some of them at close quarters and observing many from a distance. There is a tremendous opportunity for each of us to learn from our coworkers—the good and even the bad—if we are willing to accept new information. Fortunately, the almighty has blessed each one of us and has given us more positive traits than negative ones. The winning mantra is to retain our good qualities and learn from others to alter the bad ones.

You Cannot Miss the Good Ones

Some of our coworkers bring a lot of cheer and positivity to our lives. At the workplace, you not only work with each other but also inadvertently share a lot of human values and goodness. However hard you may try, keeping your personality at home and wanting to be "just business" at work is difficult. Your habits are visible to everyone who deals with you.

Some people can brighten your day, and you tend to spend more time with them, take their advice, and often even confide in them for your problems.

Several such people build relationships with us that go well beyond the workplace boundary. You miss such jolly good fellows even after you quit the organization. Most importantly, you can bank on such people much after you have left the organization. Such colleagues become our lifetime assets.

> *"At every stage of my career I have had interesting and cordial colleagues, some of whom are close friends".*
>
> —Daniel Nathans

In today's fast-paced world, such colleagues are a treasure that needs to be protected and preserved. So first thing is to become a good, likable coworker.

Colleagues Who Inspire You

Motivating a team is not done by the leader alone. Each team member can motivate their peers. Though not a part of their job profile, some colleagues inspire others by how they conduct themselves, love their job and enthusiasm. Several coworkers take pride in their jobs and often wear them on their sleeves. They inspire others in a team.

They always leverage the strength of coworkers toward a collective goal. It is up to us how we look at such sincere people. We could be jealous of them or we could envy them. You can envy such people but learn to emulate them, look up to them as your silent mentors and learn a thing or two from such great fellows.

Authoritative Yet Polite

In a complex work environment, there are wheels within wheels and gradually, hierarchies emerge. The team leader could start depending on some team members and allocate them more responsibility and a larger role. Some may misuse this and try to throw their weight around, which is often disliked by their peers. The sensible ones don't show their authority but are firm with peers yet very polite. This is a sign of maturity. Surprisingly, many people don't learn it even after sufficient experience, and several smart ones learn this quickly. Such colleagues enhance the performance of the team without stepping on anybody's toes.

Always Respectful and Well Mannered

This quality is universally appreciated and doesn't cost a penny. Yet, most of us don't have it. Good manners and measured behavior earn respect. Being too loud or haughty is not viewed positively by everyone. Simple expressions like "Thank you" or "You have been a great help" go a long way in establishing a strong bond with others.

Courageous Colleagues

In a workplace, you may not require physical courage. What is important is the courage to stand up for one's values and the tenacity to withstand pressure. One often sees people buckling down under pressure from either the environment or the bosses. Those who demonstrate professional courage and call a spade a spade are respected by their colleagues.

I have experienced situations where colleagues let you down in front of others, often taking a U-turn on the commitment they so boastfully made to you earlier. They chicken out in front of bosses as they are unprepared to stick their necks out. Such people simply pull the rug from under your feet, leaving you embarrassed. You have got to be careful of colleagues who do not display the courage to take their commitment forward.

Calm and Composed Ones

To remain calm in a crisis is not easy. Most of us can't remain composed if there is a major crisis situation on our hands. To remain calm during a crisis requires a different type of courage. This is God's gift and is conferred upon only a few. Such people become great colleagues because they act as an anchor during a storm. It is good to have such angels in a team.

Reliability Factor

In today's turbulent and materialistic times, it is very difficult to get reliable people on board any organization. If we look around ourselves, it isn't easy to find reliable drivers, peons or even a helping hand at home. There is a shortage of reliable people whom you can depend upon. It is such a boon to have dependable and committed teammates because they make your life better and stable. In a day's work, there are always situations where you require some support, assistance or help. You will always turn to a colleague who is credible, responsible and unfailing.

A colleague in need is a colleague indeed.

You Need an Honest Feedback

Each of us wants to be appreciated, patted on the back and encouraged to move forward. Many of us like it when others say what we want to hear. Coworkers say good things to each other so that the status quo is maintained. In other words, it is "You scratch my back and I scratch yours".

In reality, you need someone to point out your weaknesses.

Well-meaning colleagues are ready to make suggestions for improvement by pointing out our flaws. This is a double-edged weapon. Human nature is averse to honest feedback, and many people take such friends at work as judgmental, critical and sometimes demeaning or even derogatory. It depends on how you look at it. I feel colleagues who give us honest feedback are real friends because they want us to improve and do better in life.

Here, the trust factor comes in. You would accept feedback from only those colleagues and friends whom you trust.

Authors and actors need genuine feedback to make amends. Actors get feedback from critiques as well as the audience. As head of a management college, I used to get input from parents. I always encouraged them to give suggestions, and wherever required, I ensured that those points were implemented.

Good Colleagues Are Good Teachers Too

This is closely linked to giving honest feedback. Genuine colleagues will go out of their way to guide you wherever you want their help. This is very handy when you join a new organization. For the first few months, you are in the learning mode. You make genuine efforts to learn the ropes, but if someone helps you, it becomes easier.

I have been fortunate that every time I joined a new organization, I had very helpful colleagues.

This becomes extremely critical in technical assignments, too. I had two stints in organizations that were into software development. When you are required to work on a new operating system using a programming language that you are not very familiar with, you need people around you to be helpful. I was again fortunate to have colleagues who acted as mentors and patiently taught me.

Out-of-the-box Thinkers

Innovative coworkers are a great source of inspiration to the entire workforce. They are, in a way, troubleshooters and their expertise is called for whenever there is a problem that seems to have no solution. Whether it is the optimization of resources, rationalization of manpower or launch of a new product, these out-of-the-box thinkers can make some very concrete suggestions that save time, effort as well as resources.

Such colleagues display sheer common sense and are great simplifiers. In every large organization, I bump into a couple of them and always look up to them whenever I get stuck with a problem which I cannot handle on my own.

These pathbreakers can give you the best travel plan for your holiday and also advise you on how to get your leave approved by your boss! They are inherently very resourceful.

Many such smart fellows also demonstrate a great presence of mind.

Integrity

All of us expect honesty from our office boy, clerk and even our domestic help. Therefore, this becomes a must-have quality in the people we work with.

People at the workplace who demonstrate integrity, those who are ethical and have strong values and principles are always respected by their peers as well as their bosses. These people will never shortchange anyone for their personal gains.

There can be an error of judgment that can be accepted, but an error of intent can never be accepted.

You can measure integrity at the workplace by being observant. It could be something as small as signing the attendance register. When an employee makes a false entry by writing at the wrong time of arrival, he exposes himself as a person with no integrity. Inflating travel bills, misusing official resources for personal gains, etc., are all indicators of dishonesty and reflect upon one's integrity.

As team members, when we demonstrate ethics in our day-to-day work, it is appreciated, and it impacts the rest of the team positively.

Integrity lies in our mentality and our attitude. As they say, if you don't tell a lie, you will not have to remember anything.

Trust is the Key to Relationship Management

Trust works at two levels. First, it is the overall environment that must be perceived by every employee as trustworthy. Good organizations, through their top management, make constant, sincere efforts to create a culture with trust as its core value. It takes years to build such an organization, but it is worth the effort. Second, it works at an individual level. If two coworkers can't trust each other, then it is challenging for them to work together. For a peer-to-peer relationship to thrive, trust becomes the most critical factor. Trust between people cannot be built overnight. When teammates work together, they observe each other's behavior all the time. As a team player, it is therefore essential for one to build a bond with others on the basis of being trustworthy.

Others must be able to trust your wisdom, your professional competence and most importantly, your intentions as a fellow human being. One must remember that it takes a long time to earn the respect and trust of your colleagues, but it can get shattered with one lie or one wrongdoing. It is very difficult to build trust after it has been broken; that is how human nature works.

It is not difficult to earn the trust of your coworkers. They start respecting you and gradually even confide in you. At a professional level, it is your competence that speaks for you. For instance, you start trusting your physicians over a period of time if they have been able to help you out of your ailments every time you visit them. You trust your drivers because you have seen their driving skills over some time. And you rely on your drivers on the honesty continuum because they don't tell lies and they don't pilfer your fuel. Therefore, to earn respect as a colleague, one must be downright honest and try to be as efficient and competent as possible at one's job.

Empathy and Caring for Others

Empathy is all about caring for others and having the ability and intention to understand and share the feelings of others. Nature has given each one the ability to feel how others feel. Some of us develop this effectively, whereas some don't. Dayanand Saraswati said, "because a human being is endowed with empathy, he violates the natural order if he does not reach out to those who need care. Responding to this empathy, one is in harmony". If someone is in distress or has suffered a personal loss, his colleagues and friends play an important part in helping that person out of that crisis. Providing moral support and holding a person's hand when the chips are down for someone can do a lot of good.

Ones Who Take Responsibility for Their Work and Own Up To Mistakes

On the face of it, these seem to be fundamental and easy-to-possess qualities. Observing a little more closely, one finds that all our mates at the workplace don't own up to their mistakes.

Many do not reflect a habit of taking responsibility—especially when tasked with something specific.

People who take responsibility seriously are respected by their bosses and looked up to by their coworkers. Those who take shortcuts, sham it out and are not earnest enough lose out in the long run professionally.

It is so easy to own up to your mistake and say sorry. Yet most people are arrogant not to accept their mistakes. The whole world knows when you make a mistake; no amount of denial will help. Then why not acknowledge it? Accepting it earns you respect. You don't become small; you raise your status by being truthful about your shortcomings. This is so much against the basic ego of human beings and, therefore, difficult to practice by most people.

Allow Yourself to Be Critically Evaluated

This is also related to our inflated ego. No one wants to be evaluated by others because, while positive feedback is flattering, the negative inputs that point a finger at our weaknesses hurt us and our ego.

I remember my boss, who was professionally very sound; he used to make three or four subordinates sit through his mock presentation. The idea was to take candid feedback so that he could make his presentation better. Since he was so open to being critically evaluated, we used to give him our frank opinion. And he would listen in carefully. If he had erred, he would accept it. As a result, he earned our respect and made brilliant, impactful presentations.

Creating a Healthy Competition

It is natural to have competition among peers. Let us not pretend; no one wants to be left behind in a competitive environment. Everybody wants their next promotion; everyone wants recognition and appreciation.

Can colleagues create a "healthy" competition in such a scenario? It is difficult but not impossible. You need to be a little large-hearted to pull this one off. Healthy competition doesn't mean you let a guy walk over you. You work hard, but there should be no foul play. Fair play and equal opportunity are at the core of healthy competition. There are people in an organization or a department who will give their best shot, and thereafter, don't worry about the results.

> *"My peers and colleagues inspire me".*
>
> —Robin Chase

Intellectually Inspiring Coworkers

Such people are held in awe and looked up to by their coworkers. These are the folks who are abreast with the latest happenings. News, articles, opinions and vocabulary—you name it, and they have it. They always appear updated, confident, intelligent and better informed than others across the team. They are always impactful—even during a casual conversation.

For instance, when they speak in the cafeteria, heads turn, and people often say, "Hey, who's this person? Appears to be very updated and suave".

They can find the right words for the right occasions and are able to articulate their ideas very well, making even complex issues look very simple.

They are well-read, which accounts for all these traits. Such individuals read a lot. They would take every opportunity to learn something they are not aware of. In addition to reading professionally relevant material, they also read a lot of fiction, non-professional material, magazines and other articles.

Staying in the company of such intellectuals is not only a pleasure, but it helps in getting intellectually inspired.

Intellectuals often become opinion-makers. Bosses often consult them, and they sometimes acquire the hallowed position of an unofficial advisor of sorts.

Bouncing Back After a Personal Tragedy

Handling failure or a tragedy is easier said than done. Many of us take a long time to recover from a personal loss. As they say, "life must go on", and those who move in life make it much better for themselves and those around them.

Such colleagues leave a lasting impression on you. During your own difficult times, you can look up to them to draw the desired strength.

Real and Not Virtual

Communications and computers have stormed our lives to the extent that today, we consider them an indispensable part of our lives. It has altered the way we work and the way we communicate. Computers have made things a lot simpler, and 24x7 connectivity makes each one of us more productive. On a personal level, this has made relationships very synthetic. It has diminished the "bio" factor in our relationships. The real purpose of the interaction is lost even though these do make things simpler. People send emails and text messages to those seated in the adjacent cubicles today because we are so accustomed to doing this. In these interactions, there is hardly any warmth. It is sometimes beneficial to go back to the old school of thought and meet people face to face rather than chatting on a monitor or sending irrelevant jokes and messages on social media.

I have seen colleagues who prefer to walk over to your cabin and spend a little quality time with you. It is such a refreshing change to sit across the table and discuss the issues, which get resolved much faster than sending trail mail for the same problem. That "touch and feel" factor is something essential to human relations and is a great enabler that helps build bonds of friendship and camaraderie.

Senior members of the hierarchy enjoy casually catching up with their coworkers as they pass in the hallways. They don't mind going to the shop floor to get the "pulse" of the organization. I have worked with people who never sat firmly behind large desks but instead went outside to interact with people.

Life is not virtual, but it is very real, and living a real life has its own charm and advantages.

Professionally Competent Friends

In every organization, some coworkers are experts at their job. They are not only an asset to the organization but are of great value to people who work with them. Coupled with a positive helping attitude, these people take the role of mentors effortlessly. The coworkers automatically get attracted to them and never hesitate to take their advice or assistance.

During my tenure in an organization tasked to develop specialized software, we were all challenged to work on a new hardware platform, an absolutely new operating system, and a programming language we were unfamiliar with. We were lucky to have a few who were very clued up and helped us.

> *"It's a great honor to be recognized and appreciated by your fellow colleagues".*
>
> —Pierre-Emerick Aubameyang

Celebrating Others' Achievements

This really doesn't cost much. I see it all the time at the campus during placements. Everyone doesn't get placed on day one. On the first day of placement, every student is anxious and nervous. The pressure is tremendous, and it's a do-or-die situation for every student. Only a few lucky ones get a job offer on the first day of the interviews. The batch congratulates all who get selected, and each evening is a celebration. As days go by, more students get placed, and the time comes when only a handful are left. It is good to see that most of them, though a little disappointed, keep a smile intact. At this time, the rest of the batch comes to their rescue and boosts their morale by encouraging them and giving them tips to crack the following interview. This is an excellent example of mutual support and mutual celebration.

In organizations, others usually celebrate if someone gets a promotion. Those who don't, demonstrate their frustration and jealousy. This is never appreciated. A good coworker would and ought to be pleased with their colleague's accomplishments. Everybody wants recognition and rewards, but one should not be jealous of the achievers.

This is easier said than done. You need a lot of maturity and a big heart to celebrate what you couldn't get and what others have achieved.

Remember, it may be your turn tomorrow—when you win, and there may be no one to celebrate your success.

Those Who Call a Spade a Spade

Teammates who don't mince words are held in high esteem. They are sometimes so frank and forthright that they are considered undiplomatic or rude. I think such people are good because they don't take things to heart or keep any grudges. If you understand such people, they can be a great asset because they tell you the truth to your face. Such people rarely resort to foul-mouthing behind your back or indulge in backbiting.

The opposite of this lot is the ones I term as "too sweet for my liking." They may not actually mean what they say but will do a lot of sweet-talking in front of you.

I have come across colleagues who air their views frankly in meetings and discussions. They may sound rude, but they are well-meaning. One should go by their intentions and not phraseology.

In the real world, sometimes it's essential to be a little diplomatic. It is not necessary to be sincere to the point of hurting others. Observing frank guys, one learns to keep one's mouth shut in places. As they say, "Being transparent doesn't mean being naked"!

Colleagues Can Do a Lot of Value Addition

Coworkers are a great source of knowledge. Since I work with postgraduate management students, I have been observing this for a few decades. This hypothesis includes the idea that the batch performs better overall the more diverse it is. Since a management program is multidisciplinary, you get students from science, arts, commerce, engineering, hospitality and media, to name a few. People come from different regions of the country. In such an environment, students get ample opportunities to learn a whole lot of different things from each other. Students could learn more from each other than from classwork. Apart from academic and geographic diversity, many facts about human behavior differ from person to person. In addition, games, extracurricular activities, discussions and topics of preference also contribute to batch diversity.

It is a two-sided affair. If you want to take advantage of demographic diversity, the sky is the limit. But those who remain in their own cocoon seldom benefit.

Almost a similar situation prevails at the workplace. In today's scenario, you have people from all over the country coming and working under the same roof. You have a great opportunity to do value addition to yourself in such a rich and diverse environment, provided you want to.

Grounded and Humble

Today, everyone seems to impress everyone else. In a way, it is an artificial living where we judge our own esteem by the likes we get on Facebook. It isn't confined to our private life but also depends on our workplace. We sometimes feel that there are more show-off buffs than solid guys around us.

Yet some sane souls clearly demonstrate that they are stable, secure, in control of things and need not show off. Such people promise less but deliver more. They neither overestimate their own abilities nor do they talk big and make unrealistic plans. In a way, they are a little conservative about their estimations. Such people are a great company. They don't ever sound foolish or brag about themselves.

Such people always give a measured response to situations. Their opinions and estimates are realistic and worth considering. They will never pump you up and get into a situation you cannot handle. Given a task, they will not promise unless they are very sure of delivering. Such guys radiate confidence and inspire positivity in others. Their opinions matter to colleagues, subordinates, as well as their bosses. People listen to them intently when they give suggestions in meetings or discussions.

Let us briefly look at the most common cardinal sins some of our coworkers commit.

> *"I don't see any of my colleagues as rivals. I don't think our generation needs to do that. We are a chilled out lot, and we should all be happy".*
>
> —Shahid Kapoor

Brownie Points and Politics

The urge to score over others is a basic human instinct. If we were not competitive, humans wouldn't have made any progress. As long as the competition is healthy and you are not exaggerating your achievements to score points that you don't deserve, it's a fair game.

The problem starts, and no one likes it when you do things or say things only to impress bosses and your colleagues. Many of our colleagues resort to this approach to hide their weaknesses and incompetence.

Organizational politics is linked to this. People try to manage the corridors of power for their selfish motives. Pitching one against the other and backbiting are the most practiced and preferred tactics in office politics.

Though people blame bosses for encouraging and tolerating organizational politics, colleagues are equally to be blamed. The worst part of office politics is that it is a double-edged weapon. If your politics doesn't work, it may boomerang against you, and you can be in deep trouble. Therefore, if you want to have peace at the workplace and get your dues, just work hard, have faith in your competence and stay away from office politics.

Selfish Colleagues

The worst guy is not only selfish; he is also prepared to use you to his advantage. You need to look after your interests but not at the cost of others. People who think only about themselves are smart enough to ensure that others don't get to know about their schemes. They are good at winning others' trust through sweet talk and polite behavior. Investing your time and feelings with such colleagues is like dumping your emotions and interactions into a black hole. You can't expect anything in return.

It is not difficult to identify such people. In fact, a couple of their selfish acts are enough to expose them. The entire friend circle soon gets to know such people and starts avoiding them. These people are the least helpful and the biggest help seekers. If they need your help and if they know you can do it, they will bend backwards to seek help. Once their work is done, they would just disappear.

Values Mismatch

Best friends in the workplace are those with whom there is a frequency match. The most important is the value system of an individual. Values are beliefs that a person feels are desirable or undesirable. They differ from person to person and also sometimes from time to time. As one grows and matures, some beliefs may seem obsolete and unimportant. These values can also change with circumstances.

There was once a couple that took excellent care of their parents. The parents stayed with them. One of their friends and his wife found sending their parents to the old age home convenient. This was not liked by the first couple, who hated the idea of an old age home. Their friendship gradually fell apart as a result of this mismatch.

You get along well with people who have a similar value system. Honest people who value integrity would stay away from those who are dishonest. Conversely, people with the same value system can build a strong relationship based on shared values.

The Bootlickers

The most irritating colleagues are those who suck up to seniors. In our desi lingo, they are called *chamchas.*

Such people try to cover up their incompetence and attempt to compensate by acting as stooges to their bosses. This is one trait that divulges a lot about a colleague. A person who is incompetent and still wants to climb the ladder and get promotions could be a dangerous person to work with. To get what they want, they may be ready to sacrifice the interests of their close friends and colleagues. This tribe is not diminishing; on the contrary, you find many such people on the same floor who are incompetent yet ambitious—the diciest combination!

Identify such people and stay away.

Do We Have a Choice?

You cannot choose your neighbors. Similarly, you cannot choose your coworkers. If you have been assigned to a department, there is no guarantee who occupy the next desk. Similarly, in smaller clusters, where teams are formed for specific tasks or projects, you have very little control over who you work with.

The best way to handle such a heterogeneous crowd is that we first behave ourselves. If we are looking for good and "comfortable to work with" kind of colleagues, the others are also looking at us in the same way.

If we are good, the law of attraction will work for us—good people will get attracted to us. Therefore, it is important to get our act together first.

Once that has been done, it is time to implement our filtering process. If one is a little careful, it is not difficult to separate the wheat from the chaff. Identify the good fellows as per your yardstick and ensure you stick to this lot. Avoid those who don't meet your standards—this doesn't mean you become very snooty and choosey. Let us remember that, as per the law of averages, you will have plenty of good fellows in an organization. Therefore, identify the bad hats and try to stay clear of them.

Sometimes, you need to overlook the shortfalls of colleagues. Let us understand that no one can be perfect, so don't even look for perfect colleagues. It will be a frustrating experience.

Sometimes, you need to put up with bad neighbors too.

> *"For me, the team always comes first, and without the help of my colleagues, I am nothing".*
>
> —Ruben Neves

Selecting a Good Team

If you have a choice to recruit and assemble your own team, even then, it may not be possible to get the nicest guys on board. You may still land up with some good and some bad. That is why referral checks are done. It is not your professional competence alone that matters; your other habits and behavioral traits, as covered till now, matter a lot—maybe more than being a great, professionally competent employee.

20
Yeh Dil Maange More

"You cannot escape the responsibility of tomorrow by evading it today".

—Abraham Lincoln

In June 1999, when Captain Vikram Batra was assigned the task of capturing Point 5140, he chose his success signal to be *Yeh Dil Maange More*. Over the years, the slogan has been remembered for the courage and valor of Captain Batra, but it first came to the spotlight as the slogan of the beverage brand Pepsi had made Yeh Dil Maange More a household mantra in the late '90s.

He was evacuating an injured soldier when he was hit in the chest by an enemy sniper and, a second later, was hit by a rocket-propelled grenade (RPG). Batra breathed his last next to his fellow company man. Captain Vikram Batra was awarded the Param Vir Chakra on August 15, 1999.

Let me narrate an experience. I am happy and lucky that most of my MBA students are doing extremely well in their professional lives after finishing their MBA. Many of them are still in touch with me and often seek my advice on complex professional matters.

Two such students, now young executives working for an automobile giant in Mumbai, once came to my office. I offered them a cup of tea, and as we settled down, they wanted to discuss something they were upset about.

I had to prod them to get to the real problem. One of them said, "Sir, our boss gives us a lot of work, but our salary is less than another guy in the team who is also as experienced as us but has done his MBA from a foreign university. This seems to be unfair to us. What should we do"?

I agree that this was unfair and is a corporate problem across the board when they think and compensate for employees like this. You must understand that you cannot change the world and people's perceptions. If you complain, they will give a two-word answer, "company policy," and policy is cast in stone for them. Therefore, I asked them, "Are you happy with your boss, and is he happy with your work"?

The answer was quick, "Yes, Sir, he is pleased, which is why he depends on us and keeps giving us more and more work every day. And he appreciates in front of his boss, too"!

> *"Without hard work, nothing grows but weeds".*
>
> —Gordon B Hinckley

I said, "The catchword here is you are "dependable," and that is what matters. Ask for more responsibility and a bigger role, and things will improve automatically. Keep working hard, and things will work out".

These guys took my advice and went back partly convinced. Within the next six months, they both got an offer from Volvo, offering them twice the salary!

The Volvo brand is one of the world's best-known and respected brands within the commercial vehicle industry. It is associated with the core values of quality, safety and environmental care.

"Volvo" is Latin and means "I roll".

Their cars are top-of-the-line and very high-end.

For instance, the Volvo XC90 is a four-seater SUV available in a price range of 93.90 lakh–1.31 crore rupees.

These guys were thrilled, and their hard work and extra responsibility helped.

Another student of mine was working for a telecom company and was asking me how to do better and get a promotion. My advice was along similar lines, and I said, "Ask for bigger responsibility, a bigger circle area and a bigger challenge. Money and promotion will automatically come. The industry is looking for people who walk the extra mile". He is doing very well and was picked up by a real estate giant offering him a job in Dubai.

So, *Dil Maange More* is the formula for success.

> *"Winners embrace hard work. They love the discipline of it, the trade-off they're making to win. Losers, on the other hand, see it as punishment. And that's the difference".*
>
> —Lou Holtz

Let me share another experience with one of the toppers. This girl got placed on the first day of the campus placement program with an American IT product manufacturing company at a very high compensation.

She had a different type of problem. She was an engineering topper and wanted a technical profile but was offered a sales/marketing job! She tried to refuse that offer but sought my advice. I told her to take up the job as the company was one of the top three brands, and I was sure her talent would be spotted in due course and rewarded. She joined. Within six months, she called and said, "Sir, I have got a technical profile, and I am heading a project to develop fraud-management software for an Indian telecom service provider giant".

> *"You can delegate authority, but you cannot delegate responsibility".*
>
> —Byron Dorgan

In this chapter, there are two big learning points.

First, ask for more responsibility and more work. You will learn more, and your good reputation will travel at lightning speed. Your mantra and chant should be "Sir, *yeh dil maange* more".

Second, your talent will be recognized sooner or later, and you will get slotted into the right job best suited for you. In your first job, don't be too choosey.

21
Promise to Stay On

"Individual commitment to a group effort—that is what makes a team work, a company work, a society work, a civilization work".

—Vince Lombardi

One of the biggest problems of the business community is employee attrition. This has been happening for decades and remains fluid and fluctuates as per the economic cycle, demand and supply, and several other reasons. I was talking to the CTO of a large CSP cellular service provider, and what he told me was annoying and amusing.

He said, "I take a meeting of my technical group every Monday morning and every time, I find at least twenty-five per cent new faces! How do you work like this? You have to brief and rebrief and brief all over again"!

This is one of the biggest problems of a company that is manpower intensive. I feel it is largely the fault of employees, but not always. There are problems with the bosses and company culture, too. Today, it has become a fashion to change jobs quickly. You don't change jobs as you change your undergarments! For heaven's sake, think of the company too. This is a matter of ethics, as I see it.

Hire and fire culture is alarming. But today, employees fire themselves out! It is a two-way street.

Remember the old saying—"A rolling stone gathers no moss". It means that people who travel a lot do not accrue commitments. The proverb means that a man who is constantly changing his vocation, who cannot stick to a particular job, will never win success.

Almost fifteen years back, I was talking to the HR head of a business process outsourcing (BPO) in Bangalore, and he said, pointing his finger outside his window, "Sir, can you see that faraway building? You know, every week, a hundred employees don't turn up for work. They vanish, and do you know where and why"? I was all ears and asked him for the answer. He said, "Can you believe that for just five hundred rupees a month raise, they jump the job and go to that building with another BPO? They don't even inform us"! How bad can this get? Loyalty and responsibility are also something. What if someone fires you tomorrow without notice and puts you into hot soup? Is this ethical either way? NO.

Those days, it was a BPO boom and their HR team jokingly said, "Trespassers will be recruited"!

It is more pronounced in the IT sector and has become worse. *The New Indian Express* reports a bad situation[1]. This is the current post-pandemic, event-centric situation.

During the pandemic lot of learning and delivery by companies like Zomato, etc., picked up, and there was a sudden boom in IT services/apps to be delivered. Zoom meetings and the like became very prevalent. The need for software coders and designers shot up. Demand became high, and IT firms started poaching for higher salaries.

A record number of people have either quit their organizations or are planning to. The "great attrition" is real, and it's happening now, particularly impacting the IT industry. As companies see record attrition, now is a difficult time for managers, as they have to adapt to a cultural shift where the focus has shifted from work to workers. For months to come, all eyes will be on the bosses.

---

1. Goel, Samiksha. "The 'Great Attrition': It's a Difficult Time to Be a Boss..." *The New Indian Express*, November 21, 2021. https://www.newindianexpress.com/business/2021/nov/21/the-great-attrition-its-a-difficult-time-to-be-a-boss-2386165.html.

Spoilt for Choices

According to research firm Gartner, the attrition rate rose from 10 per cent in 2020 to 20 per cent in 2021. Some IT service providers are even battling higher attrition rates of up to 30 per cent. Another survey by the firm between May and June 2021 found that nearly half of today's applicants are considering at least two job offers.

This is the post-pandemic situation. People have left for their homes, many not returning. In general, if we take a block of a few years, things are not so bad.

> *"If you are only doing what you are getting paid for, and doing it no better than the average employee, then your pay is most likely right where it should be".*
>
> —Bo Bennett

I remember talking to a senior HR professional of a computer MNC, one of the biggest in the world, around fifteen years back regarding manpower problems and recruitment challenges. He had a similar experience that the people at the junior levels keep shifting from one company to another, and that too for flimsy reasons. When you go to a seminar, you bump into so many guys with different visiting cards than what they had during the last seminar just a couple of months ago. Can you imagine the disruption at work, especially the damage done to software development projects where continuity is extremely important?

If the employer walks a mile to accommodate talent, then talent also needs to go halfway. An employee who has an inflated market value today cannot expect every positive move from the employer alone. It ethically must be both ways, or else it amounts to blackmail or, at best, holding a company at ransom. In the end, it affects the new joinees because the recruiters look at them with suspicion, with tainted glasses—which may not be wrong.

Manufacturing Vs Services

An analysis of the difference in attrition levels between the manufacturing and the services sectors reveals many differing factors in the operation of both industries.

These lead to the difference in the rates at which employees switch jobs there.

In services, people hold more power as they contribute to a greater extent to the company's turnover. "The value-add in manufacturing primarily comes from the machinery".

Almost a hundred years ago, Walt Disney faced the same problem with his artists working for his studios. It was much worse out there because getting a good/best cartoonist was a big challenge.

According to Pankaj Lochan, the group CHRO of Jindal Steel and Power, "The nature of job in the manufacturing space results in low attrition. Manufacturing involves a process, a machine. I call it 'the causative element'. One has greater control over the cause. In case of services, the overall control over causative elements is lower".[2]

Therefore, let us not get carried away with the software sector. If everyone starts programming, who will manufacture cars, buildings, hospitals, hotels, shipping, logistics and hundreds of more jobs to build the nation? Every graduate passing out cannot be a software person, and why should they be?

We need to look at sixty-five lakh graduates wanting to do different things. In addition, a nation cannot flourish on software services alone.

Catch 22 Situation

Underemployment is even more acute in India. India's skilling problem is a classic conundrum. Young people desperately search for entry-level jobs while employers, ironically, are unable to find people with the right skills or could face a monthly turnover, sometimes as high as a fifth of their workforce. The ranks of young, often educated, unemployed people are building up.[3]

2. Akshit Pushkarna | HRKatha, "Why Do Traditional Companies Have Lower Attrition Rates?," *HR Katha*, September 2, 2021, https://www.hrkatha.com/features/why-do-traditional-companies-have-lower-attrition-rates/.
3. Rajat Gupta and Saipriya Sarangan, "Skilling India: As Unemployment Soars; Here's a Solution," *Financial Express*, July 15, 2016, https://www.financialexpress.com/opinion/skilling-india-as-unemployment-soars-heres-a-solution/317153/.

There is a shortage of IT/software professionals due to the spurt in the requirements caused by the pandemic. It would level out sooner than later. The problem may be with smaller companies to get new talent with skills and dedication.

The problem, according to my research and understanding, is complex yet not complicated. If there are no jobs, then why is there so much attrition?

This means that there are jobs for those who are good, and they ditch a company for a few dollars more!

The problem of getting a job is for those first-timers who are not good enough.

Therefore, once you get a job, make sure you stick there for at least two years if not more. One, you give stability to the company; two, you demonstrate ethical behavior; and three, you learn and mature.

Let me tell you, too many job changes don't do good for your CV.

Companies now invest a lot of time and money in training and upskilling their employees. This is true even in India. How does abandoning a company out of greed turn into ethical behavior?

> *"Recently, I was asked if I was going to fire an employee who made a mistake that cost the company $600,000. No, I replied, I just spent $600,000 training him. Why would I want somebody to hire his experience"?*
>
> —Thomas J. Watson

The present-day situation of the economy, jobs and business may not be the way to look at and become a basis of long-term assessment for job seekers—it is too fluid, and it will be wrong to base one's analysis and advice on the current situation.

However, taking a look back at the past ten years and ahead to when things stabilize, one can say with some degree of certainty that there will be lot of demand for new candidates in the near future. However, youth must prepare themselves by developing their skills and knowledge in order to become employable. No one will hand you the job; you have to earn it. Don't say, "*Sadda haq aithe rakh*" but instead "*Haqdar bano*".

Water, Water Everywhere . . . No Water to Drink

This happens when you are on a lifeboat or raft in the sea. You can't drink salty, dirty seawater, but you need to know how to create good drinkable water. You can survive without food for a week but die of thirst in three days.

In rough seas, you cannot get uncontaminated freshwater. At night, secure the tarpaulin like a sunshade and turn its edges to collect dew. Collecting dew along the sides of the raft is also possible using a sponge or cloth. When it rains, drink as much as you can hold and try to store it in a plastic bag—every drop matters.

A similar situation exists for fresh job seekers. They have to learn to get a job, make all efforts, upskill, read and invest time wisely. Once you get a job, stick to it for a reasonable time.

Never Burn Bridges When You Leave

This is a very important point to remember. There are occasions when you have to quit or are asked to quit. Whatever the case, never be rude to people when you leave. You may have some complaints or grudges, which could be genuine, but you should not spoil relationships—never burn bridges.

> "*Mend fences, build bridges, forgive trespasses, grieve losses and let toxic grudges go. Then move on*".
>
> —Unicahija Tamano

I remember almost eighteen years ago, one of my students working in a company had a problem with her manager, and she left in a huff without informing the company. She also took away the cupboard keys with her. The MD was very unhappy, and he called me up and gave me a mouthful, saying, "Such are your students". I had to apologize for no fault of mine, and my staff called up this girl (we maintain an updated database of alumni) and asked her to go and return the office keys and hand over her charge amicably, resolving this situation. Remember, a bad reputation travels like wildfire. It can become a major problem when seeking your next job. So beware!

Your reputation reaches a new company before you reach. In such a mad rush- which happens once in a while- like some sudden demand due to unforeseen reasons, it is always a good idea to demonstrate some respect and loyalty to your company. If you stick around when the company needs you, in the short run, you may feel you have lost, but your organization will definitely compensate you once things improve in the job market. Remember, humans, at the end of the day, are by and large good, and you do get your rewards in the long run. Continuity is a two-way street. You benefit because you are already a known person to all, and the company benefits as they get continuity and not a jarring experience of training a new guy.

In the long run, you will be seen as a dependable person even in a crisis, and this will help you do better in your career.

Rahul Dravid. The name itself is an institution when it comes to Indian cricket. The Wall, Mr Dependable and our man in need was the one who put his hand up when needed for the side. Yes, for sixteen years, he has been the silent saviour, and despite playing in Sachin Tendulkar's shadow for his entire career, he has still left a legacy to be proud of.[4]

4. Adhikari, Somak. "Rahul Dravid, Team India's Wall And Mr Dependable, Did Whatever The Side Needed Him To." *IndiaTimes*, January 11, 2023. https://www.indiatimes.com/sports/rahul-dravid-team-indias-wall-and-mr-dependable-did-whatever-the-side-needed-him-to-506058.html.

22
How Can You Contribute to the Culture of Your Organization?

"The thing that I have learned at IBM is that culture is everything".

—LV Gestuer, former CEO, IBM

Before I discuss how employees, especially at the entry-level, contribute and why they should do this, let me explain how much effort is put in by top management and promoters to create a solid culture and why.

How do you differentiate a good organization from a bad one? The one-word answer to this is "culture." Work culture is the organization's intangible ingredient, which makes it tick. The top management and especially the leaders of organizations have to make sure that setting their organization's culture right is at the top of their priority list.

I would not like to go into the technical definition of culture but would put it in simple words. "Organizational culture is how an employee feels about the organization". Do employees feel happy and motivated or do they just come to work to draw their pay? The organization is not brick and mortar, but it is the flesh and blood of the people who work there. You may feel very motivated and happy working in a small restaurant as a manager but may feel suffocated in a five-star hotel as a lobby manager because of bad work culture. Culture is invisible to the eye but can impact your heart and soul. It is like pure oxygen, which is not visible but is essential to even walking or sitting down on a chair.

The first thing is that every employee should have faith in the organization that they work for. Leaders or powers that be must, therefore, build an environment of trust. In addition, everyone should have some sense of security. This doesn't mean that people will get paid and retain their jobs whether they work or not. It means that if a person does their job sincerely, they need not worry about their job or their promotions or remunerations. People must find that they are in a professional environment where they are paid for performance and not for invisibles like caste, creed, color or favoritisms. It should be a free space to work where everybody should be able to breathe freely.

Politics, if played in an organization, can mess up the culture of an organization. You may do whatever you want for the welfare of your employees, but if you play politics, all of it will go down the drain.

These, in my view, come under the best practices of a company. If people believe in me, why do I need a suggestion box outside my office? They should be able to walk up to me and project their problems, and I, as a leader, should be able to give them some satisfactory answers. In none of the organizations I have worked for have I had to resort to a suggestion box!

> *"The only thing of real importance that leaders do is to create and manage culture. If you do not manage culture, it manages you".*
>
> —Edgar Schein

I was giving a talk at a forum, and while talking about culture, I said that Tata was a company that had a very ethical way of working and provided a suitable environment for its people to work. People, therefore, didn't leave them quickly. During the question-answer session, one gentleman said, "Sir, I retired from Tata last year after working for forty years. I pray to God that in my next birth also, I should work for Tata—you are so very right"! There was a big applause from the audience.

This is the power of culture. "People don't leave organizations; they leave bad organizational culture"!

A leader must ensure that everyone is treated fairly, with no double standards, favorites and partiality. Practicing all this doesn't require any effort.

What differentiates a good and a bad educational institute? Here again, culture is the main differentiator. It is more pronounced in the case of management institutes. All of them have a computing facility, a library, good faculty, a cafeteria and an auditorium, but why one is doing better than the other? Here also, a good culture makes the difference.

My own experience tells me that top leadership requires a lot of effort to set up a good culture in the organization. But once it is in place, it creates a great work environment. It is easy to instill a good culture when the organization has just been established. Changing the culture of an organization that has been in existence for decades is a very difficult task. This, I feel, is the greatest challenge for a leader who takes charge of a sick unit or not-so-healthy organization.

Out here, the brick and mortar are not rotting, but the people and their minds are. To turn around a company, one has to turn around the culture, and you will see spectacular positive changes very quickly. My advice to start-ups is to establish a good culture from day one; it is much easier to do that. I have lectured at many places where I addressed principals and heads of educational institutes on "How do you make an educational institute vibrant and ticking"? At the end of the lecture, people came and told me that they had been in the business of education for so very long but never realized these things, which were so easy to implement.

A good, vibrant organization ensures that people stick to it, and you may well be surprised that attrition reduces to a large extent. It increases the organization's overall efficiency and makes people more effective. A good culture is like a pot of honey that will attract good employees to join you. As a leader, your job is to make people proud of being a part of your team, and a good culture does precisely that.

Remember, "Every drop matters".

If one can start trusting people, I am sure we will have a large number of good and honest people. Somewhere deep down, everybody has a conscience. It is a matter of give and take, and it indeed works.

> *"The way management treats their associates is exactly how the associates will treat the customers".*
>
> —Sam Walton, Founder, Walmart

What Can You Do to Contribute to the Culture, and Why Should You?

Culture is like one spoonful of good curd that you add to one liter of milk, then leave for the night, and the following day you get one liter of lovely curd! That is the power of culture.

- Everyone wants to get a raise or a promotion, but very few are those employees who ask, "What can I bring to the organization"? They don't know that knowing how to add positive vibes and culture to your company is the first step to getting a raise or promotion. If you want to be first amongst equals, you should cash on this, which most people don't understand. You can become the most significant invisible contributor.

Employees who know how to add value to their jobs and the culture of the organization tend to command higher salaries, more exciting projects and better job opportunities. Such people are hard to find, especially today when ethics and honesty are often compromised for materialistic gains. Organizations, big or small, value employees like this so much that they'll do everything possible to keep that person, even in a recession, layoff or merger.

Remember, if the culture is set by top leadership, it is implemented by all employees, especially those at the middle and bottom of the pyramid. Also, keep in mind that the bottom of the pyramid is the broadest and is the foundation on which everything stands for centuries.

- Let us say you work hard, and your manager knows that you also motivate others to work harder, so it goes a big way in your favor. But if you discourage others from working hard or worst ask them to take a shortcut, you become a bad egg who spoils the rest, too.
- Let me quote a recent example. PM Modi started a Swachh Bharat Mission, an effort toward a cultural shift. He said in so many words that we take baths every day to keep ourselves clean and our homes clean, but we do not keep our society and cities clean. Even though there are government and municipal bodies in charge of keeping the streets and public spaces clean, each person's contribution is what matters most because there are 1.4 billion of us. Constant reminders, in terms of advertisements, have helped, but without the contribution of every citizen, it would not have been possible.
- Many employees go about their professional lives equating the years of service they put into the value they give. This may work in the public sector, but the corporate world doesn't work like that.
- Don't get involved in politics or backbiting. This can finish your career.
- Don't create camps or group-ism and become a ring leader of sorts to impede the work of the organization and dampen productivity.
- Instead, join groups that contribute to the betterment of coworkers and the company. You may start a "yoga initiative", a debate club, a book reading club or a football team, just like in your college days. That is why those who are active in extracurricular activities in school and college are taken in for the job in the first place.
- One important thing is to understand what the top management has set cultural pointers as values and then first follow them and also take these things forward. For instance, if your company's top brass takes pride in the

timely delivery of things, then you must work for this and also think of ways you can improve on this.

> *"My fellow Americans, ask not what your country can do for you, ask what you can do for your country".*
>
> —John F Kennedy

Therefore, think about how you can do good things beyond your job description to contribute to the positivity of the work culture.

23
Stress Management for Professionals and Students

Thousands of books, research papers and articles have been written about how to deal with stress, yet we all experience significant amounts of stress. There are strategies for managing stress that have been developed by almost every university and every professional organization, but there is not a one-size-fits-all approach or mantra that can be used to handle stress quickly.

The majority of experts, books and research focus on ways to manage stress, which means how to handle stress after it has built up and lessen its impact on you personally. This is very crucial because stress is an inevitable part of a typical workday.

What is Stress?

Job stress is described as harmful emotional responses that can be felt by a person when the requirements of the job do not match the capabilities and resources of the worker. Job stress can lead to poor health, feelings of panic, and being overwhelmed by forces you cannot control.

I want to focus in this chapter on two fundamental ideas. First, we should avoid unnecessary stress levels to build. Second, how can you lessen its impact on you if it still affects you, which is certain despite your first?

Let us deal with on-the-job stress in this chapter.

What is Stress Management?

Stress management is creating and using methods, ideas, strategies or techniques that reduce stress and the adverse effects of stress on your mental or physical well-being. A variety of ways are there that can be used to manage stress. These include cognitive, emotional and behavioral control.

Stress and Pressure

Pressure is usually from outside and refers to external expectations to perform, deliver or over deliver. At the same time, stress refers to the internal feeling of being unprepared, overloaded or overwhelmed due to a lack of knowledge or resources.

Stress is what you feel when you have three assignments to complete in two days, and you do not have enough time.

The organization or your boss pressures you to do things faster than you can deliver.

Organize Yourself to Become More Efficient

Remember, prevention is better than cure.

Many of us are disorganized—some are bad as a habit, and some don't bother to think it is a very good habit that empowers you to do better. Remaining organized is no rocket science—it is just creating a habit of doing things methodically and efficiently.

If you are organized at work, you may save two hours in a work day of eight hours, which improves your efficiency and lets you work at peace with yourself. If everything around your workspace goes according to how you want, you are in control of things and begin to enjoy your work. If you are, on the contrary, working in a haphazard way, you will be building stress for yourself; you may feel helpless running around things that could have been avoided.

You are preventing stress from building on you in the first place. Don't waste time looking for your wallet or car keys at home in the morning; you waste time and energy and get a foul mood as a bonus.

You must create a 'to-do list' prior to the beginning of the day. Some people do it in the morning before heading to work! The best time to do this is in the morning when no one is around to disturb you and you are fresh at home.

Take a notebook and write down all that needs to be done in the coming day; you may carry forward yesterday's pending points to add to the list.

Make Goals and Revise Them When Necessary

There are three most important tasks. Write down and make a mental note of your top three tasks to get done for the day. Everything else seems to fall into place if you do that.

- Make lists and prioritize them as A, B or C. A being most urgent and important.
- Manage your time well by not gossiping or avoiding time wasters like long calls. This is a habit of most young workers; if you can finish a call in 3 minutes, don't unnecessarily stretch it to 10 with pleasantries and chatter.
- Use calendars, planners and alarms as reminders, if required.

Do one thing at a time.

Multitasking is a fashionable word. But humans are better performers for one task at a time. Doing several functions at a time creates stress and may negatively impact your quality of work.

Do It Now! Don't Delay! Don't Procrastinate!

As a habit, clear your desk before you leave from work.

Make use of the word no. You cannot keep everyone happy. Sometimes, you should say, 'no, this cannot be done'.

Delegate tasks. This is very important. Some people, by habit, try to do everything themselves. In all good organizations, tasks are cut out as per your Job description. Stick to these, and if something has to be done by a colleague, hand over that task to him.

Manage Your Emails According to Priority

Reduce clutter. Organize your workplace and table, however small—the smaller, the better. There should be a place for everything, and everything must be in its place. Find places that are easy to get to for all the things you use most often. Do not forget your charger at home. If needed, have two—one for home, one for the office, and the same for reading glasses. They don't cost very much.

The simplest thing you should make as a habit is to put whatever tool, item, clothing, bag, pencil, pen, etc. away immediately after using it. You will always know where everything and anything is, so you never waste time looking for something. Very efficient. A hallmark of great habit.

Simplify, Simplify, Simplify!

This is very important; make it a habit. If you have a task, find the simplest way to simplify presentations and discussions.

Get Along With People—Make Friends at Work

People go to the office as they meet people. Covid work from home had its advantages, but people missed office culture. We were taught in school that 'man is a social animal,' which is so true. School kids missed their friends, too.

You should not isolate yourself; instead, find a few trustworthy, like-minded friends. They indirectly serve as stress relievers as well because you can talk about some of your issues and seek solutions. Talking to people one to one, face-to-face, is so much more human than chatting on mail or mobile.

You Cannot Choose Your Boss

Like they say, you cannot choose your parents. Understand what your boss thinks and what are his likes and dislikes, follow them and keep the glass cool.

Become accustomed to things. Don't forget you are also a boss to someone. What kind of work would you like your subordinate to do for you—and what should you be doing for your boss? Human relations can make or mar your day's work.

Laughter—The Best Medicine

Hope you have a good sense of humor; if not, try to develop one. This is very important. Nothing soothes you more than a good joke told at an appropriate time. Make friends who are jovial, lively and not always stiff-lipped.

Monitor Your Stress—First Identify Your Stress Triggers

After you have done all of the above, stress is creepy and will raise its ugly head occasionally. You need to keep a watch. What triggers stress for you? Avoid such situations if you can. Deflecting is a better strategy than buying stress.

Telltale Marks of Stress Building on You

These are certain things that could happen when you are stressed out

- Tense or painful muscles and feeling tired all day long.

  Possibly experienced in the shoulders, back, chest, stomach or head.
- Digestive issues

  Nausea, vomiting, diarrhoea and constipation.
- Faster Heartbeat and high blood pressure

Releasing of stress hormones (adrenaline) can impact heart rate and blood pressure.

Each physical indicator can become part of our self-awareness and may suggest when stress gets out of hand. When stress builds up, your behavior changes.

- You start jumping to conclusions
- Ability to problem solve and move forward is curtailed
- Casting blame on others often
- Overgeneralizing and hyper behaviour
- Overreacting to situations, leaving us anxious and overwhelmed

Avoid using Alcohol or Drugs to Manage Stress

This should never be done because it only serves to exacerbate the issue.

Therefore, take care of the following:

Sleep

Sleep is something you cannot shortchange on. Must sleep at least 6 to 8 hours in a 24-hour day. It repairs your body and mind.

Mobile phones are a big disturbance; put them on silent mode and don't keep checking messages at night.

Diet

If you aim to manage stress, eat enough nutritious food to fuel all your body's systems.

Exercise

Going for long walks is the best stress buster. This is the best bet if you have a green patch of trees or a garden.

Some More Tips to Handle Stress

- Use some form of time management and use it regularly. This will give you more control over what you spend your time and energy on. There are short courses available and some simple books too. These can be of immense help.
- Reduce procrastination. Although everyone procrastinates, the more you can overcome this, the less stressful your life will be. Letting a significant project wait until the last minute is incredibly stressful but ultimately under your control.
- Try setting small goals each day.
- Write down all of the things you have accomplished once a day, no matter how small they\may seem. This boosts your morale and self-confidence, which will also improve your performance.

Positive Self-talk helps

We all talk to ourselves, especially if no one is watching us! Self-talk can be positive ("I can do this" or "everything will be OK") or negative ("I'll never get better" or "I'm so stupid"). Negative self-talk increases stress. Positive self-talk can help you calm down and manage stress. With practice, you can learn to shift negative thoughts to positive ones. For example:

- Instead of saying to yourself, "I can't do this", say, "I'll do the best I can".
- Instead of saying, "I get upset when this happens", say, "I know how to deal with this–I've done it before".

- Do this at every possible time you can. In your workplace, at home, in a lift alone or in your car.

Deep Breathing and Yoga Help

Find a quiet location if possible.

- Inhale slowly through your nose while silently counting to 3.
- Hold your breath for the count of three.
- Exhale slowly through your nose while silently counting to 3.
- With your breath expelled, count to three.
- Repeat the cycle several times.

Join a yoga class; it is good for physical health, too.

Some More Little Things That Can Help

Here are some stress relievers:

- Count to 10 before you speak or react. It enables you to compose.
- Take a few slow, deep breaths until you feel your body unclench.
- If it's not urgent, sleep on it and respond tomorrow. This works especially well for stressful emails and social media trolls. When angry, you might write nasty emails that can hurt later.
- Walk away from the event or the storm troubling you, and handle it later once things calm down.
- Break down big problems into smaller parts. This is a good way to make the problem look manageable. Take one step at a time.
- Work out or do something active. Exercise is an excellent antidote for stress.
- Indulge in stress-busting activities like walking, running or riding a bike to clear your head.

Most Important Parting Shot

We get stressed because we constantly think of 'what will be the consequences'?

If you lose a wad of notes worth, say, 100,000, you cannot take any meaning full action because you are so scared of losing that much money. If you accept this loss in the worst case, what will happen? We get over-concerned about minor issues and magnify them as if heaven will fall!

One good way is to do the following:

- Write down what the problem is. Once you write down, there is clarity, and you do not exaggerate.
- What are the consequences? At most, I will not get the money back.
- Accept the consequence in the worst-case scenario. Even if I don't get this back, I can manage the loss over the next three months.
- Now you are relaxed and say what best can be done to manage the problem.

24
How to Become a Star Performer

"Star performers are my favorite to manage and lead. Star performers are critical to any organization, and the key is how can you capture their heart-share and their mind-share when they're on this fast track".

—John Stumpf

How can you become the blue-eyed starlet of your bosses and be loved by the management? Let me tell you it is not difficult to be liked and appreciated by your management. You have people around you, your coworkers, your friends and the entire young lot, which today is looking for only a salary raise, promotion, and chilling out. They do not want work; they want a job and a hefty salary, and on top of that, they want appreciation! Tell me, if you are running even a tiny shop of garments and your salesperson makes ten mistakes a day, doesn't tell you how much of sales happened, keeps sitting the whole day, doesn't inform you if someone important called in your absence, doesn't tally the items marked in a box that you ask him to count, does not attend to a walk-in customer, or refuses to show different items, will you like it? No, not at all. On the other hand, another salesperson is attentive all the time, keeps you informed about customer feedback, gives a report of sales on his own before shutting shop, and completes the work given by you on time. Would you not like to appreciate that person? Yes, I am sure you will.

You Are There for a Purpose

Please remember that every organization takes a headcount of people they employ. Your salary comes from the profits the company makes. Therefore, you are not required if you do not contribute to the profits. It is that simple. Secondly, you are there to assist the manager, supervisor or the boss. You are there to make their job simpler and share some of the workloads. Is this rocket science? No, it is common sense. Why are some people liked by employers and some are not? A manager wants sincere, hardworking and responsible people. No one likes a casual "I don't care" type of attitude—whatever may be your job profile. If you are paid, you need to perform. If you excel, you are further rewarded.

Information is Power and Comforting

During my workshops, I always advised my participants to keep their superiors informed by keeping them in the loop. Don't just vanish. If a task is assigned and, for example, it must be completed by 6 p.m., you are expected to complete the work and submit a completion report. Good employees typically complete it earlier than expected. I had a personal secretary who was very professional and responsive. She would complete her work well ahead of schedule and notify me immediately that it was finished. In her three years working for me, I never had to ask about the task's progress. I was not happy when she had to quit the job because of family obligations. Anyone would like to have such a person working in the organization.

What should you do if, despite your best efforts, you are unable to complete your task and need more time due to circumstances that are beyond your control? There is a simple action called an "interim report". You must inform your boss that for whatever reason, you will require one more hour or, if need be, tell them 80 per cent of the work has been done, and you need half a day more and seek their permission to submit by lunchtime tomorrow. A reasonable person may even sit late into the night and do it before returning home. Such people become indispensable assets and are seen as star performers.

> *"If we did the things we are capable of, we would astound ourselves".*
>
> —Thomas Edison

Do Before You Are Asked to Do

Some people anticipate the work or a task that needs to be done regularly per their job profile. For example, suppose in a library, fifty new books have arrived. In that case, the librarian must take charge and finish the required formalities of sticking a card jacket at the end of the book and updating the records on the computer system as soon as possible. Why should the boss need to inspect the library and point out why the job was not done? A once-in-a-while lapse can be accepted, but a routine attitude of slackness will not be accepted. Therefore, do a job before you are instructed to keep your table clear; this is greatly appreciated, and people will comment on how efficient and responsible you are.

I say, "Don't work to live but live to work".

Have You Done Something Beyond the Call of Duty?

If, during your annual appraisal, I were to ask you, "What wouldn't have happened in the organization had you not been employed"? Can you give out a couple of things you did that were not routine? Let me take the example of a college library or a corporate library once more. A librarian could take pride in saying, "I got twenty books as a gift from an NGO by requesting some contribution. Or got it at twenty per cent price for a hundred books from a book mela, which appeared as an advertisement in the newspaper".

> *"The highest levels of performance come to people who are centered, intuitive, creative, and reflective—people who know to see a problem as an opportunity".*
>
> —Deepak Chopra

This is being proactive. And these points are very valuable in building your respect and getting appreciation. Just doing your job for which you are paid doesn't make you a star performer.

Bibliography

Agencies. "Sleeping Habits of Seven Most Powerful People." The Economic Times, February 11, 2017. https://economictimes.indiatimes.com/nation-world/sleeping-habits-of-seven-most-powerful-people/barack-obama/slideshow/57098129.cms.

Brookings. "The Forgotten 3 Billion | Brookings," October 25, 2022. https://www.brookings.edu/blog/future-development/2022/10/21/the-forgotten-3-billion/.

Carol Dweck, *Mindset: Changing The Way You Think To Fulfil Your Potential* (Hachette UK, 2012).

Chimnani, Neelima. "| Femina.In." Femina, April 23, 2020. https://www.femina.in/gossip/celeb-buzz/inside-srks-library-4520.html.

Christine M. Riordan, "We All Need Friends at Work," Harvard Business Review, August 7, 2014, https://hbr.org/2013/07/we-all-need-friends-at-work#:~:text=Gallup%20found%20that%20close%20work,we%20are%20in%2Dit%20together.

Crew, Bec. "Just 2 Weeks in The Mountains Can Change Your Blood For Months : ScienceAlert." ScienceAlert, October 17, 2016. https://www.sciencealert.com/just-2-weeks-in-the-mountains-can-change-your-blood-for-months.

"CRITICAL THINKING Definition & Usage Examples | Dictionary.Com," in *Dictionary.Com*, January 24, 2021, https://www.dictionary.com/browse/critical-thinking.

Desk, Entertainment. "Ketan Mehta Recalls Shooting for Shah Rukh Khan's First Film When the Actor's Mother Was in 'Critical Situation': 'He Was Full of Energy'" The Indian Express, July 5, 2023. https://indianexpress.com/article/entertainment/bollywood/ketan-mehta-recalls-shooting-shah-rukh-khan-first-film-.

Dickens, Greg. "The Most Ignored Advice from Steve Jobs (and How It Can Be Your Secret Weapon)." Medium, June 20, 2018. https://medium.com/swlh/the-most-ignored-advice-from-steve-jobs-and-how-it-can-be-your-secret-weapon-3995c51d54fc#:~:text=%E2%80%9CIt's%20in%20Apple's%20DNA%20that,to%20making%20Apple%20so%20successful.

Farboled, "Education Indoctrination - Writing 150 Fall 2020 - Medium," *Medium*, December 16, 2021, https://medium.com/writing-150-fall-2020/education-indoctrination-c339ddab0755.

Garfield, Simon, and Special To Cnn. "One Thing We Owe to Steve Jobs." CNN, October 6, 2011. https://edition.cnn.com/2011/10/05/opinion/garfield-steve-jobs-fonts/index.html.

Goleman, Daniel. Emotional Intelligence: Why It Can Matter More than IQ, 1995. http://ci.nii.ac.jp/ncid/BA28658620.

Gupta, Rajat, and Saipriya Sarangan. "Skilling India: As Unemployment Soars; Here's a Solution." Financial Express, July 15, 2016. https://www.financialexpress.com/opinion/skilling-india-as-unemployment-soars-heres-a-solution/317153/.

"Hiring Challenges In The FMCG Sector Explained," n.d. https://www.scantec.co.uk/blog/view/279/index2/Hiring-Challenges-In-The-Fmcg-Sector-Explained.

"How Henry Ford Became Rich | Melbado," n.d. https://melbado.com/how-henry-ford-became-rich/.

HRKatha, Akshit Pushkarna |. "Why Do Traditional Companies Have Lower Attrition Rates?" HR Katha, September 2, 2021. https://www.hrkatha.com/features/why-do-traditional-companies-have-lower-attrition-rates/.

"6 Important Critical Thinking Skills You Should Master," n.d., https://www.betterup.com/blog/critical-thinking-skills#:~:text=a%20better%20learner-,6%20key%20critical%20thinking%20skills,to%20the%20critical%20thinking%20process.

Jj. "Camelot: Once There Was a Spot: A Love of Words~ J.Jones." Camelot: One Brief Shining Moment, February 24, 2021. https://pastprettie.wordpress.com/2021/02/24/camelot-once-there-was-a-spot-a-love-of-words-j-jones/.

Kakutani, Michiko. "Obama's Secret to Surviving the White House Years: Books." The New York Times, September 17, 2020. https://www.nytimes.com/2017/01/16/books/obamas-secret-to-surviving-the-white-house-years-books.html.

Lalit K Jha and Pti, "'Indian and Chinese Students out-Competing US with Hard Work,'" *Www.Business-Standard.Com*, January 19, 2013, https://www.business-standard.com/article/economy-policy/-indian-and-chinese-students-out-competing-us-with-hard-work-110012800115_1.html.

Lee A. Iacocca and Sonny Kleinfield, *Talking Straight* (Bantam Books, 1989).

Miller, Zoë. "14 People Who Turned Their Hobbies into Million- and Billion-Dollar Careers." Insider, November 15, 2018. https://www.insider.com/million-dollar-hobbies-careers-2018-6#mark-zuckerberg-facebook-6.

"Mosquitoes Resistant to DDT Are Also Resistant to Mosquito Net Insecticide," n.d. https://www.biomedcentral.com/about/press-centre/science-press-releases/25-feb-2014.

Navidad, Angel E., and Angel E. Navidad. "Marshmallow Test Experiment and Delayed Gratification." Simply Psychology, August 18, 2023. https://www.simplypsychology.org/marshmallow-test.html.

Piecing Together the Poverty Puzzle. Washington, DC: World Bank EBooks, 2018. https://doi.org/10.1596/978-1-4648-1330-6.

"Poverty Facts and Stats," January 7, 2013. https://www.globalissues.org/article/26/poverty-facts-and-stats.

Pti. "India Has Highest Number of People Living below Poverty Line: World Bank." Business Today, October 3, 2016. https://www.businesstoday.in/latest/economy-politics/story/india-has-highest-number-of-people-living-below-poverty-line-world-bank-69179-2016-10-03.

Quast, Lisa. "How Becoming A Mentor Can Boost Your Career." Forbes, October 31, 2011. https://www.forbes.com/sites/lisaquast/2011/10/31/how-becoming-a-mentor-can-boost-your-career/?sh=47772b835f57.

Randewich, Noel, and Tiyashi Datta. "Apple's Market Value Ends above $3 Trillion for First Time." Reuters, June 30, 2023. https://www.reuters.com/technology/apples-market-value-breaches-3-trillion-mark-again-2023-06-30/.

Reuters. "Factbox: Tech Giants Dominate Wall Street's Trillion-Dollar Club." Reuters, December 9, 2021. https://www.reuters.com/markets/europe/tech-giants-dominate-wall-streets-trillion-dollar-club-2021-12-09.

Santa Clara University, "Facebook and Our Fake News Problem," n.d., https://www.scu.edu/ethics/focus-areas/business-ethics/resources/facebook-and-our-fake-news-problem/.

Sengupta, Pallav. "Health Impacts of Yoga and Pranayama: A State-of-the-Art Review." PubMed Central (PMC), July 1, 2012. https://www.ncbi.nlm.nih.gov/pmc/articles/PMC3415184/.

Somak Adhikari, "Rahul Dravid, Team India's Wall And Mr Dependable, Did Whatever The Side Needed Him To," *IndiaTimes*, January 11, 2023, https://www.indiatimes.com/sports/rahul-dravid-team-indias-wall-and-mr-dependable-did-whatever-the-side-needed-him-to-506058.html.

Steger, Charles. "Why Do We Need the Humanities?" The Conversation, n.d. https://theconversation.com/why-do-we-need-the-humanities-38640.

Torres, Libby. "15 Reasons Fans Believe Keanu Reeves Is the Greatest Person Ever." Insider, November 26, 2022. https://www.insider.com/keanu-reeves-greatest-person-ever-2019-8.

WebDesk, ZeeBiz. "Google Parent Company Alphabet Eyes Elite $2 Trillion Market Valuation after Blowout Results." Zee Business, February 3, 2022. https://www.zeebiz.com/world/news-google-parent-company-alphabet-eyes-elite-2-trillion-market-valuation-after-blowout-results-177971.

Wikipedia contributors, "Speed Reading," Wikipedia, October 16, 2023, https://en.wikipedia.org/wiki/Speed_reading#:~:text=Kennedy%20was%20a%20proponent%20of,of%201%2C200%20words%20per%20minute.

Yussuf. "Reading vs Watching Videos: What Science Says - Digital Minimalism." Digital Minimalism, April 27, 2022. https://digitalminimalism.com/reading-vs-watching-videos-what-science-says/.